"Using the latest research in brain science and cognitive psychology, *Mind Your Mindset* will show you how your mind is placing limits on your success—and how to remove them! I highly recommend this book."

Tony Robbins, #1 *New York Times* bestselling
author, entrepreneur, philanthropist, and
the world's #1 life and business strategist

"Is your mind holding you back or moving you forward? *Mind Your Mindset* teaches you how to change your thoughts in order to make the changes you want in your life, along with the science behind how to make those changes last! I highly recommend this book!"

Jamie Kern Lima, *New York Times* bestselling author of *Believe It*

"I've known Michael and Megan for years, and they embody the principles in this book. Honest, thoughtful, compelling, and highly practical, *Mind Your Mindset* is a must-read."

John C. Maxwell, bestselling author, speaker, and coach

"All of us know about the little voice inside our heads. What we don't know is that much of what it tells us isn't true! *Mind Your Mindset* is all about changing the narrative of your life. Change the story, change the outcome. This approach really works."

Francesca Gino, author of *Rebel Talent* and
Harvard Business School professor

"Your story is powerful, especially when you take control of the narrative. Choosing to change your storyline can be the difference between a broken and a blessed life. Michael and Megan will show you how science and strategy can help reshape your thinking, tell better stories, and get greater outcomes."

Dave Ramsey, bestselling author and radio host

"Michael Hyatt and Megan Hyatt Miller are friends of mine, and they have written a terrific book. *Mind Your Mindset* is going to inform, inspire, and encourage you to get inside your head so you can get out of the way in your life. This book will help you figure out what's got you stuck and give you practical tips on what you can do about it. You'll be glad you read it."

Bob Goff, *New York Times* bestselling author of *Love Does*

"The old saying 'It's all in your head' is way more true than we often understand. Our brains make maps of ourselves, others, and the world. If we do not intentionally make sure those maps are accurate, our lives will suffer and be limited. But when we do, incredible possibilities open up that we never have experienced. Thanks, Michael, for this great reminder!"

Dr. Henry Cloud, *New York Times* bestselling
author and psychologist

"Your brain is a storytelling machine. My friends Mike Hyatt and Megan Hyatt Miller can show you how to program it to tell better stories, stories that lead to a better ending in your business and personal life. Positive change is within your reach! Go and get it!"

Ian Morgan Cron, bestselling author of *The Road Back to You*

"As a serial entrepreneur with ADHD, I know firsthand how limiting negative beliefs can be. This book will help you understand how the stories we tell ourselves often create our greatest limits. You'll love the actionable steps it provides to change those narratives and unlock your highest potential, peak performance, and most importantly, free your mind from worry. Filled with science, stories, and strategies, this book has the power to change the trajectory of your life. . . . The Hyatts have done it again!"

Chalene Johnson, *New York Times* bestselling author; business
and lifestyle expert; motivational speaker; and podcaster

"*Mind Your Mindset* asks a crucial question for diagnosing a problem: 'What story are you telling yourself about this situation?' With honest reflection, your options for better action immediately expand. Get this book and learn to make better, faster decisions and actions."

Dr. Benjamin Hardy, organizational psychologist
and bestselling author of *The Gap and the Gain*

"As a creative person with a mind that often runs away, I wrestle with controlling my thoughts on a daily basis. That's why I am so thankful for Michael Hyatt and Megan Hyatt Miller's new book, *Mind Your Mindset*. Michael and Megan not only empower you with fascinating science behind how the brain works so that you can control your mind, they show you exactly how to do it in practical and actionable steps. This book will set you free from the onslaught of (often negative) thoughts weighing you down every day. Everyone needs to read this!"

Christy Wright, Ramsey personality

"There is a reason that some of the greatest business and leadership books of all time share a common concept: think. *Think and Grow Rich*, *As a Man Thinketh*, etc. *Mind Your Mindset* is likely to become one of those all-time greats. Michael and Megan explore how our thoughts, more than anything else, drive our results. The principles and practices in this book, many of which I've learned from working with Michael over the years, will help anyone achieve more than they thought possible. I'm a fan of all of Michael's work, but this may be his, and Megan's, best yet."

Cody Foster, cofounder of Advisors Excel

"Scientists have described the standard, unchallenged thinking of humans as 'cow paths in the brain.' These familiar paths often keep us from seeing all there is to see. *Mind Your Mindset* will show you how to form new neural pathways in your brain to break out of the old, proven stories that hold you back and limit your progress and achievement. If you're feeling trapped or like you just stepped in something mushy, and you think the whole world stinks, it's likely you are simply on a 'cow path.' This book will push you beyond your current thinking and challenge the limits of common sense."

Dan Miller, author of *48 Days to the Work You Love*

"*Mind Your Mindset* is a must-read for anyone who desires to improve the results they are getting in business and life. After having invested the last few decades in coaching and leadership development, I have to say that the content of this book focuses in on the very foundation of human transformation. This book can be a game changer for you!"

Daniel Harkavy, author and founder and CEO of Building Champions and SetPath

"Michael and Megan clearly and powerfully apply cutting-edge neuroscience and decades of personal experience to offer solutions to the challenges our own mindset creates. Looking to change your perspective in entrepreneurship, parenting, personal growth, or leadership? Start by reading *Mind Your Mindset*. Their case studies are gripping. Their insights spot-on. It's the go-to guide you've been looking for!"

Emily Balcetis, author of *Clearer, Closer, Better: How Successful People See the World*

"This book is so needed, especially at a time in our culture when there are so many warring narratives hijacking our happiness. The quality of life you live is related directly to the story you tell yourself. *Mind Your Mindset* will help you find a better way to live: with greater freedom, purpose, and contentment. There's a lot here—don't miss it!"

Jeff Goins, bestselling author of *Real Artists Don't Starve*

"So often when we experience dreams that don't come true, or challenges in work or relationships, we feel discouragement and a bit of helplessness. We don't know the next step, or if we should simply give up the dream and move on. But using the latest neuroscience and their own vulnerable personal narratives, Michael and Megan show that we have so many options in our minds that we never allowed ourselves to consider. What is more, they provide clear and immediately actionable steps to get you and your brain on the right track to success. Highly recommended."

John Townsend, PhD, *New York Times* bestselling author of the Boundaries series and founder of the Townsend Institute

"You win in the mind first. Then you win in business and life. The mind is like a garden. You must weed the negative and feed the positive in order to produce great fruit. That's why I love this book and believe everyone should read it! It gives you the tools to elevate your thoughts, which will elevate your career, impact, and life!"

Jon Gordon, 12-time bestselling author of *The Energy Bus* and *The Garden*

"Change your thoughts, change your results. It's really that simple. Michael Hyatt and Megan Hyatt Miller's new book, *Mind Your Mindset*, will teach you exactly how to understand your thoughts in a way that works for you and your goals. From this, you will be able to achieve anything you want! Managing your mind is one of the most important skills every high achiever must master. Thanks to this new book, we now have the tools to make it happen!"

Julie Solomon, business coach, author, and host of *The Influencer Podcast*

"The stories we tell ourselves shape everything. In this practical and thought-provoking book, Michael and Megan challenge us to write new stories, so we can get our dreams out of our heads and make what matters happen in all spheres of life."

Laura Vanderkam, author of *Off the Clock* and *168 Hours*

"This book takes the complex world of brain science and makes it approachable. If you're wanting to learn more about your mind, how it works, and how it drives your actions, this is the book. Truly a blueprint for personal growth."

Lewis Howes, *New York Times* bestselling author of *The School of Greatness*

"The quality of our life is determined by the stories we tell ourselves. But instead of us shaping our stories, they end up shaping us. If you want to escape this trap—if you want to change your story and write a better one—this book is essential reading."

Ozan Varol, bestselling author of *Think like a Rocket Scientist*

"Ordinarily, I read a book with a yellow highlighter and pen close at hand. Not this time. Michael and Megan have written a remarkable book that must be experienced. Viscerally. Not studied or examined. Or outlined. Or just posted about. When I do read it again (which I will), I'll have my marker and pen. But this time I soaked in the luxury of it. Here is wisdom beautifully expressed. And insight brilliantly unpacked. And heart-pounding inspiration. Read it. Then, read it again. You will not be disappointed. Thank you, Michael and Megan. Count me among the very grateful."

Robert Wolgemuth, bestselling author

"When it comes to achieving your goals, there's no skill more essential than mastering your mindset. Michael and Megan have done an incredible job of breaking down the science of how our brains work, and how that science affects the stories we tell ourselves.

What an amazing approach to creating positive change in your business, relationships, and life!"

"*Mind Your Mindset* has the power to unlock the barriers to your success and unleash your greatest potential."

"If you are interested in learning how to think better so you can achieve better results in all aspects of life, then *Mind Your Mindset* is a must-read. Through their own stories, Michael and Megan bring complex concepts to life in a thought-provoking yet simple way to help readers change their thoughts and improve their outcomes."

"The biggest enemy many of us face as we chase our goals is . . . our own mind! Packed full of insightful stories and helpful research, *Mind Your Mindset* is a practical playbook for reclaiming your inner narratives and busting out of mental ruts."

"In this book, Michael Hyatt and Megan Hyatt Miller help you understand the inner workings of your mind so you can see reality clearer and find better, more creative solutions to achieving your goals. You'll come to see uncertainty, unsettling as it may be, as possibility, and you'll be free to create new and more effective solutions to the problems you face in business and in life."

MIND
YOUR
MINDSET

MIND
YOUR
MINDSET

The Science That Shows Success
Starts with Your Thinking

MICHAEL HYATT AND
MEGAN HYATT MILLER

BakerBooks
a division of Baker Publishing Group
Grand Rapids, Michigan

Published by Baker Books
a division of Baker Publishing Group
PO Box 6287, Grand Rapids, MI 49516-6287
www.bakerbooks.com

Printed in the United States of America

Library of Congress Cataloging-in-Publication Data
Names: Hyatt, Michael S., 1955– author. | Hyatt Miller, Megan, 1980– author.
Title: Mind your mindset : the science that shows success starts with your thinking /
    Michael Hyatt and Megan Hyatt Miller.
Description: Grand Rapids, MI : Baker Books, a division of Baker Publishing Group,
    [2023] | Includes index.
Identifiers: LCCN 2021043092 | ISBN 9780801094705 (cloth) | ISBN 9781540902146
    (paperback) | ISBN 9781493433971 (ebook)
Subjects: LCSH: Intentionalism. | Motivation (Psychology) | Goal (Psychology) |
    Self-realization.
Classification: LCC BF619.5 .H929 2023 | DDC 158.1—dc23
LC record available at https://lccn.loc.gov/2021043092

Scripture quotations are from THE HOLY BIBLE, NEW INTERNATIONAL VERSION®, NIV® Copyright © 1973, 1978, 1984, 2011 by Biblica, Inc.® Used by permission. All rights reserved worldwide.

Some names and identifying details have been changed to protect the privacy of individuals.

The authors are represented by Alive Literary Agency, 7680 Goddard Street, Suite 200, Colorado Springs, CO 80920, www.aliveliterary.com.

Baker Publishing Group publications use paper produced from sustainable forestry practices and post-consumer waste whenever possible.

23   24   25   26   27   28   29   7   6   5   4   3   2   1

To Ilene Muething and Arleta James

CONTENTS

PART 3
IMAGINE: Train Your Narrator

ONE

The Brain That Tells Itself Stories

When my husband, Joel, and I (Megan) decided in 2011 to expand our family through adoption, our dreams outpaced our preparation. We had almost no idea what we were signing up for.

I'd been to Uganda years before and felt drawn to adopt from that country. The process took a while, but we were matched with two amazing boys—a three-year-old, Moses, and a one-year-old, Jonah.

Two months before we were supposed to bring them home, we heard that Jonah was in the hospital with malaria. Joel and I were at the movie theater when the message came through from the babies' home director. My mama bear came out immediately. We left the theater a few minutes later and began changing our travel plans.

I never did see the end of that movie. I flew out the very next day.

Thank God everything turned out okay with Jonah. We had a friend living in Uganda who was a nurse, and she was able to help out until I arrived. But malaria was only the beginning. I'll stop there to let the boys tell their own stories. For now it's enough to say that complex, early-life trauma leaves a mark.[1]

Not going to lie: Things were really challenging with the kids in-country. And, contrary to our expectations, it only got harder when we got home. We had behavioral problems we could scarcely understand.

We started by trying what we already knew as parents. And let me just say that didn't work so great. Some adoptive parents reading this know exactly what I'm talking about. It wasn't long before we were running out of solutions, and the challenges were ramping up.

"I don't think we can do this," I told Joel one evening in tears. "This isn't working." I felt stuck on a desolate road, stranded somewhere between discouragement and despair. We weren't giving up—no way that was happening—but we also had no idea how to move forward.

My dad (Michael) always says that resources tend to show up when you're ready for them but usually not before. And sure enough, within days of that perfectly timed breakdown, I heard about Karyn Purvis, a researcher and developmental psychologist who had co-created Trust-Based Relational Intervention (TBRI).

I also found out she was speaking that week to a group of social workers, and the venue was close enough for us to attend! My mom stepped up to watch the boys overnight, and Joel and I headed to the conference.

We didn't know what to expect. I remember feeling uneasy on the drive from Nashville to Knoxville, like I was actively trying to restrain my hopes. It didn't feel safe to hope. I just knew we needed help. By then, we'd long since blown past the limits of our own best thinking.

We walked into the convention room with nothing but notebooks, pens, and hope against hope we'd finally get some answers. And we did.

Everything we heard was new to us—and a massive relief. Dr. Purvis described situations and children that sounded just like our own. We learned that pretty much everything we'd been trying so far was bound to fail. And she had years' worth of research and direct experience to explain why.

"Kids from hard places," as Dr. Purvis called them, need another approach. There were several reasons, but one was so simple that it all clicked the minute she said it—the brain.

The Brain Is the Key

During healthy, normal development, a child learns to successfully live and adapt in the dynamic world of interpersonal relationships and environmental change. All that learning is wired in the brain through countless neural pathways and patterns, which constitute the child's repertoire of skills and abilities.

But experiences can be both formative and deformative. Trauma disrupts helpful neural patterns and creates unhelpful ones. Those disruptions produce counterproductive coping strategies and behaviors. Suddenly you're getting calls from preschool principals and household items are in pieces— along with your expectations for a life presentable enough for Instagram.

If you can't figure out how to adequately relate to people and changing circumstances—which pretty much defines what a healthy, successful person does—you're in trouble. And so are the people around you.

This truth goes way beyond my precious boys. It goes to the crux of this book and why I suspect you're reading it. It's this simple: Achieving our goals and experiencing the results we desire comes down to working with the people in our lives and the constantly changing circumstances we find ourselves in.

And your primary tool in that endeavor? Bingo: it's your brain.

Thanks to my kids and Dr. Purvis, I began an unplanned research binge on trauma and the brain. I'd always been interested in psychology, and in my twenties, I even toyed with the idea of becoming a therapist. But now the needs of my children were reigniting dormant interests and fanning the flames with restless urgency.

I embarked on a crash course in neuro-everything, trying to understand the brain, how it struggles and heals, and what I needed to know to help my boys. I'm not an authority on the brain—far from it—but I sure have read and consulted a lot of experts.

What I realized in that learning process is that all sorts of challenges people face—in fact, nearly all of them—are essentially (1) based in the brain and (2) evident in the stories we tell ourselves about reality.

I could see that in my boys. Thanks to the trauma they'd experienced, they had developed unhelpful—mostly implicit—thought patterns and stories about themselves, family, and the rest of life that led directly to behavioral difficulties.

And here was the real difference maker: I could also see the same basic problem in Joel and myself. Past experience taught us what effective parenting supposedly looked like. But our assumptions were wrong. What worked with our older kids didn't work with Moses and Jonah. The old strategies didn't fit the new context despite apparent similarities. Our thinking was incomplete and, in some cases, actually backward.

Some version of this dynamic is true for all of us. Our brains make faulty connections based on prior experience or something we picked up from others along the way. And those faulty connections show up as unhelpful stories and strategies that prevent us from experiencing the results we want.

We'll unpack that process as we go, but for now let's just say it's true for me, for you, for the teams we lead, the business leaders we interact with, and the people we see at church, the grocery store, the gym, the farmers' market, the bank—basically, everyone in all places and circumstances.

Now let me (Michael) take you back to a moment, one among many, where I learned this lesson for myself.

Out There vs. In Here

Early one August many years ago, I (Michael) was meeting with my executive coach, Ilene. I was then CEO of Thomas Nelson, one of the world's largest English-language publishing companies at the time (now part of HarperCollins). We were meeting in part to discuss the company's financial performance the prior month.

"So how did July end up?" Ilene asked.

The truth was, not great. We missed our budget. I was disappointed, and so was the entire executive team. We had worked hard to hit our numbers. But we fell short. It happens. I mostly wanted to put it behind me and move on. Still, what else could I say?

"We missed our plan," I admitted.

"Why did you miss?" she asked.

"Well, the market is tough right now," I said, and I was ready with a full explanation. I had all the facts to back up my case. "Gas prices are up. So are interest rates. This has taken a bite out of discretionary spending. Consumers are just not frequenting bookstores like we had hoped."

I wasn't done. I cited the US Census Bureau, *Publishers Weekly*, and other industry publications. I then finished with what I thought was a note of optimism: "We didn't do what we had hoped, but we're still ahead of last year."

Not bad, right? Believable? Well, my coach wasn't buying.

"Okay," Ilene said, "I get that all those things were factors. The environment is tough. But let's be honest. It's always tough, right?"

I didn't know where she was going with this, but I agreed. Yes, it's always tough. Then she dropped a bombshell on my psyche:

"Mike, what is it about your leadership that led to this outcome?"

"Excuse me?" I replied, knowing full well what she had just asked. Ilene gently repeated the question. I think I was speechless for a full two minutes. "Well, I'm not exactly sure," I stammered. "That's a great question, but I don't know quite what to say."

Thankfully, she gave me a little help.

"As long as the problem is 'out there,' you can't fix it," she said. "You're just a victim. I'm not trying to shame you. I am trying to empower you. You can't change your results until you accept full responsibility for them."

I nodded, still unsure I liked what I was hearing. But over the next few hours we worked through the question and the issues it raised. I began to realize that the story I was telling myself about reality had created a fixed horizon of possible responses.

Here I was, eager to close the chapter on July and move into August. But by imagining our performance was primarily limited by market conditions ("out there"), I was already limiting the range of possible strategies available to my team and me ("in here").

As long as the main troubles were gas prices, interest rates, and consumer behavior, we couldn't do much. The story I was so satisfied with a moment before was suddenly unpalatable to me. We had created an out for ourselves, but at the same time we had also erected an accidental barrier. My narrative about our performance in July was going to hamstring our performance in August. That realization hit me, as I said, like a bomb.

Where did that narrative come from? It seemed totally true, self-evident. But in reality it was only partially true, and my team and I went to some effort to assemble the evidence to confirm the story.

We all have moments like that, don't we? We think we understand a problem or a circumstance, only to realize that we've got it wrong. These kinds of narratives become especially problematic when they block our path to our goals—when they prevent us from achieving the results we want.

Yes, there are problems "out there." But how we respond to those problems is entirely "in here"—in our own heads. We're distorting the facts, missing the facts, or putting the facts together in ways that don't really fit reality. And our crummy story somehow works for us—until we realize that it doesn't work at all. Our best thinking turns out to be a dead end.

Neurons and Narratives

One of the challenges Joel and I (Megan) faced with our boys was finding the best way to help them heal from the trauma they'd experienced. Among her recommendations, Dr. Purvis advised nutritional changes to encourage healthy brain chemistry.[2] We followed that regimen and found it helpful. But nutrition could take us only so far.

Around that time, I chanced on a book by Sebern Fisher called *Neurofeedback and the Treatment of Developmental Trauma*.[3] Neurofeedback relies on the remarkable ability of the brain to "rewire" itself—what's called neuroplasticity—to develop new and more helpful neural patterns. If trauma junks things up, neurofeedback sorts it out and puts the brain in better shape.

By the time I'd finished reading the book, I knew it was our next step. But how to take that step? If you know me, you won't be surprised that I just looked up Fisher's number and called her.

I got her voicemail. The recording said she wasn't taking new clients and wouldn't respond to messages. Undeterred, I left a message anyway. And out of the blue a few weeks later, Fisher called back!

She reiterated that she couldn't help us directly, but she put me in touch with Arleta James, an attachment therapist who specializes in helping kids from hard places and who was using neurofeedback—sometimes referred to as brain training.

We began neurofeedback, and it proved tremendously helpful. Within weeks and months we saw dramatic improvements. But neurofeedback wasn't the only tool in Arleta's kit.

Addressing neurochemistry through diet and neural patterns through neurofeedback are important. But these direct means are only part of the picture. It turns out there are other ways to train your brain, including telling and retelling our stories.[4]

There are mysteries to the human brain that may never be unraveled. But contemporary neuroscience, cognitive science, and related fields shed a tremendous amount of light on the brain and how it works.

Let's mention four key insights that will shape the conversation in the pages ahead:

1. Our brain contains a massive network of nerve cells (neurons) connecting and communicating across synapses.
2. Those neural connections both *are* how we think and *shape* how we think.
3. Those connections produce memories of the past and predictions of the future; we can think of these memories and predictions as stories.
4. Those stories inform how we see the world and act within it, including how we pursue our goals.

In other words, neurons make narratives—and our narratives determine how successful we are in achieving our goals. Storytelling is a function of how our brains conceive and represent reality, and our results depend to a large degree on how good our storytelling is.

We shouldn't be surprised by this. Stories are core to how humans think and work in the world. We rely on narratives to make meaning so we can act meaningfully.

Myths and origin stories, for instance, are attempts to establish that something is true now because something else happened before. Likewise, science and problem-solving are just forms of storytelling: *If I do* x, *then* y *will happen*. A hypothesis is simply a story about the way the world might work.

Neurons make narratives—and our narratives determine how successful we are in achieving our goals.

Some of the most effective counseling, therapy, and business and life coaching we've ever received comes down to helping us sort out our stories. And when our company, Full Focus, coaches business owners and corporate teams, part of what we're doing is offering better, more effective stories.

We are wired both to tell stories and to perform the stories we tell. But that wiring is also where we most often go wrong. How? By accepting and acting on unhelpful stories. The hard part is that this is usually not obvious to us when it would be most helpful to know it's happening.

The Invisible Step

High achievers sometimes suffer from an action bias. Maybe you can relate (we certainly can). As high achievers, when we encounter problems, gaps, or obstacles en route to our goals, we usually size up the problem quickly and jump to the solution, the strategy, like this:

Problem → Strategy

When trying to attain a new state, achieve a desired end, or improve the current situation, our usual approach is to ask if we are doing the right thing, doing it well, or doing it enough. We ask, "What can I *do* about this?" Then we devise a plan. We default to action.

And that approach usually works. If you're more than marginally successful, you've gotten pretty good at sizing up problems. Your strategies are likely to work, and you can fine-tune them to optimize your results without too much trouble.

Because this works most of the time, we assume that success mostly depends on strategy and execution. This is why productivity systems fly off the shelves. People imagine they can perform their jobs better if they learn the right tips and tricks. And there's nothing wrong with that. In fact, it's essential. But it's also insufficient.

Improving strategy and execution can take you only so far. Once you've optimized your strategy and improved your execution of that strategy, you may still be left with a gap.

That's where we get stuck: trying to solve problems in our health, relationships, or workplace by doing things that no longer work, but doing them with more energy and attention—as if oomph and drive is all we're missing.

We need to take a step back. Rather than thinking about what we're doing, we need to think about our thinking. We are missing something beyond oomph and drive; we're missing the story we're telling ourselves about the problem itself.

Problem → Story → Strategy

Our story about the problem will always determine our strategy and, with it, our results. We have to understand the nature of the problem to solve it effectively. This is where our action bias can hurt us. Our stories are sometimes invisible to us, or nearly so.

Problem → Story → Strategy

Our strategies, whatever they turn out to be, will always be based on our underlying story about our situation. So to create an effective strategy, we must have an accurate understanding of reality. Or at least accurate enough to serve us well—a little overconfidence can sometimes be a good thing.

Stories drive strategies, and strategies drive results. We need to foreground the story the same way a scientist foregrounds their hypothesis:

Problem → **STORY** → Strategy

Then we will be able to expose where our stories are coming from and when they're not serving us well, which provides the chance to tell a different, more empowering narrative.

That's what happened when my (Michael's) coach dropped her bombshell question. She exposed my story. Before that moment, I couldn't see how the narrative was functioning on my understanding of our challenges, or how it was undermining our performance.

It felt like a simple and convincing description of past reality, not a figment that defined the limits of possibility in my present and future reality. My coach's question exposed my story for what it was—less an explanation of what happened, more of a disempowering excuse about the past that robbed my team and me of agency in the present.

That's why we find when we're coaching business clients, or receiving coaching ourselves, that the most helpful thing to do is question the stories we're telling ourselves about the situation we're in.

A new story presents a bridge over the gap, a better solution to our problems. If we want better results, we have to tell ourselves better stories. And that takes us back to the brain.

Stuck in Unhelpful Stories

Narratives are not just the product of our neurons. The influence runs both directions. By changing our narratives, we can change our neural patterns, and this opens up a whole new avenue for personal growth and healing—not to mention problem-solving and innovation.

If our stories determine our experience of reality, we can improve our reality by improving our stories. And that creates a positive feedback loop that "rewires" our brain, making us stronger, more resilient, and more capable of addressing the choices, changes, and chances of life.

Let's say you picked up this book because you've got a problem, and you don't like any of the solutions you've seen so far. It could be a business problem, a personal problem, a relationship problem, any kind of problem. You're stuck on a goal—maybe several.

Or maybe you're successful by most any measure but have a nagging sense you're settling for less than your full potential. You're the kind of person who's always looking to stretch and grow, curious about what's possible next.

The answer to getting unstuck or jumping to the next level is the same: it comes down to the story you're telling yourself about your current reality—and that story is based in your brain.

The brain hosts a network of neurons—100 billion, give or take. As a point of reference, that's roughly the number of stars in the Milky Way. And each neuron connects with some 1,000 other neurons in various parts of the brain. That makes for 100 trillion neural connections.[5]

Stories, and all the thoughts that compose them, are the result of those connections. This means the number of stories we might entertain—and thus the strategies we could employ—are practically infinite.[6]

Journalist Steven Johnson offers this comparison: "There are somewhere on the order of 40 billion pages on the Web. If you assume an average of ten links per page, that means you and I are walking around with a high-density network in our skulls that is orders of magnitude larger than the entirety of the World Wide Web."[7]

But if there's practically no limit to the number of thoughts we can think, why do we so often get stuck thinking the same unhelpful thoughts or creating bogus barriers to achievement— for instance, assuming one parenting solution will work for all kids, or preparing for lackluster financial results because we can't control market conditions?

Why do we get stuck this way? One of the insights the two of us gained from both brain science and professional and personal coaching is that, as people, we're largely unaware of where our thoughts come from and how they affect our subsequent thinking and problem-solving.

Much of our unhelpful thinking has already been done for us. Our brains are masters at labeling problems, which they do mostly in the vast background of our subconscious minds. As a result, we take most of our thoughts for granted. Our brain presents them to us as settled facts, and we never think more deeply about them—even when we really need to.

The solutions to problems can seem straightforward and obvious based on our prior experience. It's easy to assume, for instance, a chronically late employee is dealing with an attitude problem. Or soft sales reflect a lack of effort by the sales team. Or the client isn't returning messages because he's uninterested. We've experienced it before, we think, so we know what to think and do in this case too.

This happens somewhat subconsciously. And we're correct often enough—or close enough—to be generally successful with our assumptions. But what do we do when those paths our brains know so well don't lead us where we want to go?

We take it all the way back to the source.

Three Steps to Extraordinary Results

As psychologist Timothy Wilson says, "We are all observers of our own behavior and draw conclusions about ourselves by watching what we do," and that includes the stories we tell and enact.[8] So when our stories are leaving us in a rut, we need to rethink our thinking.

How? We adopt a different vantage point, examine the stories our brain is telling, and imagine better, more empowering narratives. In this book, we propose a simple three-step method to accomplish this:

First, identify your problem and your story about it. Improvement begins with awareness. I (Megan) couldn't even start getting my boys the help they needed until I identified what I was already doing that was working at cross purposes.

If you've read this far, congratulations! You've already begun this step. You're now aware that these sorts of stories are automatically formed in the brain; they're influenced by positive and negative experiences, including trauma; they simultaneously facilitate and limit our responses to our environments; and we can improve our results by improving our stories.

In the next chapter we'll continue this process by examining how and why brains build narratives and why it's impossible to avoid them. We'll introduce you to the Narrator—if this book has a villain, this is it. But as we'll see later, it's also a surprising and helpful ally. Then in chapter 3 we'll show how and why the Narrator sometimes gets things wrong.

Second, interrogate the story. Neurons make narratives, but as we've seen they can make faulty stories. We need to separate what's factual from what's merely opinion, inference, conjecture, and the like. There's far more of that stuff rattling around in our heads than you might think.

In chapter 5, we'll explore how to challenge our stories. That process can be unsettling, as we'll see in chapter 7, but it's worth it.

When I (Michael) told my coach my story about missing the month, I had all the facts. But I assembled those facts—and excluded others—to arrive at a convenient but ultimately unhelpful conclusion. Once my coach and I identified and challenged my story, I was able to see reality in a new and more advantageous light.

This isn't always comfortable. Sometimes our intuitions lead us to assume our conclusions are certain. Challenging them can feel risky. But as we'll see, our success often depends on our willingness to accept the discomfort of uncertainty while we press toward better solutions. And that leads to the final step.

Third, imagine something that works better. Once we've exposed our faulty stories, we can use our brain's natural ability to rewire itself to find new paths and solutions.

These solutions often require us to look outside ourselves, to draw upon the help of our spouses, friends, teams, coaches, and other external sources for insight and new stories. Very often, the solutions we need are found not in one moment but in following a chain of new insights and next steps, like I (Megan) needed in getting help for our boys.

The rest of the book will explore how we can maximize these opportunities and attune our minds to make the connections faster and more reliably in the future.

When you understand how your brain's network functions, where your thoughts come from, how they shape your decisions, and where they can go wrong, you can reprogram your network, train your brain to tell more helpful stories, create better solutions, and experience extraordinary results.[9]

Mind Your Mindset

This book is about understanding the inner workings of your mind, which enables you to see reality clearer and find better, more creative solutions to achieving your goals.

What problem has you stuck? What change would you like to see in yourself? In your business? In the world? You can take control of your thoughts, discover creative solutions, and experience extraordinary results in your life. But there's also a risk here.

Our lives dip into ruts because, frankly, our brains often prefer familiar tracks to wide-open spaces. The brain finds safety in the familiar, so it relies on the tried-and-true neural connections that have always worked before. What's more, we're biologically wired to avoid uncertainty, and it can feel existentially threatening to question the basic nature of problems we've dealt with for years.

But there's good news: all of that can change as you understand how our minds work and how to think better, more creative thoughts.

Mind Your Mindset is your invitation to step boldly into a new and better way of thinking and living. Unsettling as it may be, uncertainty is not the enemy; it points not to chaos but to possibility. To have the confidence to engage the world and reshape our stories as needed is a far more valuable and reassuring asset than is certainty.

Once we accept the inevitability of change, we have no need to remain tied to ineffectual strategies and actions. Instead, we can respond effectively to whatever comes our way.

Of course, the reverse is also true. We can also refuse to engage in the dynamic process of rethinking and imagining new solutions. But where would that approach leave kids who need parents to experiment with better strategies? Where would that leave businesses that need leaders capable of envisioning better solutions?

More directly: Where would that leave you—right now—with whatever challenges you're facing today?

We offer you this invitation. Will you accept the challenge of uncertainty, resist the fear that would keep you passive, embrace an attitude of possibility, challenge your stories, and imagine new and more empowering narratives? Extraordinary results in work and life are on the other side of your *yes*.

True, that decision will require that you continually interrogate your experience and ask whether what you believed yesterday remains valid and helpful today. But it will also free you to become a different person than you were yesterday, and to achieve things tomorrow that seem impossible today.

Unsettling as it may be, uncertainty is not the enemy; it points not to chaos but to possibility.

There is no more exciting and satisfying way to live. And it's within your grasp. The chapters ahead will help show you how to get there.

ACTION

Think about one problem or opportunity you want to work on as you read this book. Download the Full Focus Self-Coacher at fullfocus.co/self-coacher and write it down, so you can come back to it as we progress.

PART 1

IDENTIFY

RECOGNIZE YOUR NARRATOR

TWO

Introducing the Narrator

Over the decades I (Michael) have attended thousands of conferences, talks, and lectures. I've heard powerful presenters and poor ones, excellent communicators and terrible ones.

I speak publicly, too, so I'm always interested to see how speakers perform. Whether I'm sitting in the audience or off-stage awaiting my own turn, I'm taking notes. Usually, I'm focused on the content. But I also pay attention to the delivery and technique. Is there something I can learn to do better—or not do at all?

One case stands out to me. I recall hearing the CEO of a major corporation present at a leadership conference. He started off by saying, "I'm not really a gifted speaker," and then spent the next hour painfully proving the point.

He rambled, followed tangents, abandoned trains of thought, reversed himself. He was, as one of our colleagues would say, "a hot mess express." He obviously did little to prepare, and he definitely didn't practice. As I scanned the room, there were as many people looking at their phones and the exit signs as the stage. I felt terrible for him.

But it was also inevitable, wasn't it? He warned us he wasn't any good. And he seemed to have internalized that message before stepping onstage, transforming it into a self-fulfilling prophecy.

He didn't expect much from himself and, as a result, didn't bother preparing. After all, what good would it do? He didn't have "the gift"—whatever that means. The CEO had fallen victim to what we call the Narrator; it lives inside each of our heads, narrating the events of our lives in real time. It also reviews past events to make sense of them, and looks ahead to help us deal with whatever's coming next. But sometimes the Narrator is a saboteur.

I (Megan) have my own version of this story.

WHEN I WAS GROWING UP, communicating in any way before groups and audiences scared me out of my mind. It started in high school when I felt my voice shake in front of the class and the wash of anxiety come over me. My Narrator, trying to keep me safe, told me that speaking was somehow dangerous.

My dread worsened when I watched a friend run out of a presentation during our senior year. She was afraid. I found her in the bathroom as she sobbed humiliated tears. I never wanted that to happen to me.

In my twenties, I avoided using my voice in front of groups at all costs. I couldn't even read Bible passages aloud with my small group of six to eight people. Every time I tried, I felt like I was being strangled.

I intentionally shut myself down at every professional opportunity involving any kind of speaking. To my own detriment, I stayed quiet in meetings. I passed on promotions when speaking was a job requirement. I quit writing professionally when I realized a published book would necessitate public speaking, and I declined to share in masterminds and other groups, even when I knew I was the expert. I suppressed my voice to avoid the certain panic of speaking in front of others.

The Narrator said if I spoke up or stepped onstage I would fall apart and be humiliated. Worse, the Narrator said something was deeply wrong with me.

I'm not gifted.

I'm bound to fail.

It's dangerous to stand up and speak.

There's something wrong with me.

Where do stories like that come from? In this chapter we'll identify the Narrator and show how and even where it operates in the brain. We'll see how the Narrator shapes our understanding of the world.

And we'll start by looking at one of the world's oldest stories, where a curious discovery awaited an Israeli American cognitive and computer scientist named Judea Pearl.

Where Are You, Adam?

If you're Jewish, Christian, or Muslim you're probably familiar with the story of Adam and Eve. It's a foundational narrative for all three religions. And the story has seeped far enough into popular culture that even people of other faiths and the non-religious share awareness of it.

The story of Adam and Eve is about our first parents violating God's ban on eating from the Tree of Knowledge. But Pearl noticed something else when he read the account—something peculiar about the way our minds seem to work.

Pearl first read the story as a child at school in Israel. Students there read the story several times a year. But Pearl's discovery didn't emerge on his first reading, or his second, or even his third.

"As I reread Genesis for the hundredth time," he says, "I noticed a nuance that had somehow eluded my attention for all those years."[1] You probably know the story. See if you can spot what Pearl did.

God plants the Tree of Knowledge in the middle of the garden of Eden and commands Adam to abstain from its fruit. The serpent tempts Eve to eat the forbidden fruit, which she does and then shares with Adam, who then eats as well.

Soon enough God comes looking for the pair and asks a simple question: "Where are you?" Notice that God's question calls for a fact—specifically, a location. So we might expect Adam to answer, "Over here," or "Beside the third date palm on the left." But Adam doesn't answer that way.

Instead of *where*, Adam answers *why*. Instead of a bare fact, he offers an explanation. "I heard you in the garden," he says, "and I was afraid because I was naked; so I hid."

God follows up with a pair of additional questions: "Who told you that you were naked? Have you eaten from the tree that I commanded you not to eat from?"

Again, these are simple questions about facts. Adam might have said, "Well, yes, I did eat the fruit. As for being naked, I pretty much figured it out by myself after that."

But Adam dodges the questions and replies with yet another causal explanation: "The woman you put here with me—she gave me some fruit from the tree, and I ate it."

God then turns his attention to Eve. "What is this you have done?" he asks. Pretty straightforward. The simplest answer would be, "I ate the fruit and then gave some to Adam." But Eve, too, answers *why*. "The serpent deceived me, and I ate."[2]

The story presents a curious pattern. Adam and Eve both go beyond requested facts to offer explanations. What's the significance?

Early on, says Pearl, "we humans realized the world is not made up only of dry facts (what we might call data today); rather, those facts are glued together by an intricate web of cause-effect relationships." What's more, he says, "causal explanations, not dry facts, make up the bulk of our knowledge."[3]

Human beings have an elemental need to establish meaning, to understand and explain *why* things are the way they are, *why* we do the things we do, and *why* other people do the things they do.

But most of the things we know aren't facts; they are the opinions, assumptions, and conjectures—the stories—we tell ourselves about the facts. We can't help it. Our brains are wired to establish cause-and-effect links between concepts.[4] We are wired for narratives, and the easiest place to see this is observing little kids.

How Babies Learn to Love Barbecue

The world is a strange and bewildering place for baby humans. Each of us enters the world with default programming and hardwired instincts. But beyond the ability to breathe, a basic trajectory for growth, and the desire for security, we're pretty much helpless.

We have no experience and, therefore, no understanding of how things work. We don't know that stoves are hot, cats have claws, or that—no offense, Memphis, Austin, or Kansas City— the very best barbecue in the world is in Nashville. We have to learn all of that. And most of us do.

Right now the two of us get the joy of seeing this learning process in Megan's daughter and Michael's granddaughter, Naomi. As of this writing, she's just two years old and vacuuming up new ideas faster than we can track. She's always surprising us with the connections she's making between one thing and another.

Granddaddy ("Gandy" to her) has a boat. When we talk about going to the lake, Naomi says, "Gandy boat." Notice she has three concepts here: Gandy, boat, and lake. And she's assembled them in a certain way: There's a boat, it's somehow related to Gandy, and both Gandy and the boat are usually at the lake when we go.

This sort of thing pops up all the time. At bedtime, for example, she starts mentioning the titles of books she likes and says, "You read the book." When I (Megan) tell her to say please, she corrects herself and says, "You read the book, please."

Bedtime, particular books, their titles, asking nicely: Naomi's learning process reflects an on-the-fly acquisition of concepts, connections, and the contexts in which she experiences them. It's the same for all of us.

Think about the last time you learned a new task at work, used a new app or device, or met someone new for coffee. When you encounter something or someone new, you gain new concepts, learn how they connect and work together, and you're doing so in the context of a particular project, platform, or relationship.

How does it all happen? The brain is linking ideas together in a daisy chain of neurons.

CONCEPTS ARE THE PRIMARY HANDLES we use to get a grip on the world. We form concepts when the synapses in our brain—that is, the connections between our brain cells—link neurons in specific patterns.

We have neurons whose primary job is to help us label and keep track of everything in the world and what we assume about it. Neuroscientists refer to these as concept cells. "We have networks of concept cells for people, places, things—even for ideas such as winning and losing," says science writer and physicist Leonard Mlodinow.[5]

Babies and toddlers like Naomi are constantly looking and listening, touching and tasting, because they're acquiring new concepts at a furious pace. Eventually, those concepts will be labeled by parents, friends, teachers, and others. But even before others name what we observe, our brain is busy trying to make sense of all the information it encounters.

Whenever we encounter something in the real world, our brain categorizes it, labels it, and stores it in our neural network for later access. These can be concrete things like a rock, cup, shoe, or paycheck. They can also be abstractions like love, fear, beauty, or justice.

"Every concept we ever conceive takes the physical form of a constellation of the neurons in a concept network," says Mlodinow. "They are the realization, in hardware, of our ideas."[6]

This Leads to That

Of course, concepts alone wouldn't do you much good. If all you have are seemingly random experiences, objects, and ideas shooting through your neural network, you couldn't do a lot with them. But a string of concepts connected in cause-and-effect relationships is useful.

This is what thinking is, more or less: bringing two concepts together in a relationship. Whenever we encounter something new or curious, startling or captivating, our brain riffles through our library of existing concepts and tries to make connections to what we already know.[7]

We might have to stretch an idea to fit, or string it together with other ideas, or split it into component parts. But by using what we already know, we're able to learn more. "By stringing such thoughts together," says Mlodinow, "we are led to conclusions."[8]

When Naomi drops food from the table, she gains a concept: food drops. When Joel, her dad, tells her no, she gains another concept: prohibition. Even before she has a label for these ideas, she has some sense of how they fit together.

She has created a meaning that connects the two concepts. Now she has the conceptual patterns in place to tell herself a story about the future when she tosses food again.

This is why kids ask so many questions once they gain any degree of verbal fluency. Curiosity displays their drive to connect ideas and discover the underlying logic between concepts. Harvard education professor Paul Harris estimates children ask roughly 40,000 explanatory questions between ages two and five.[9]

Stories naturally emerge from all these acts of discovering, linking, and situating: memories of what happens when you approach a task a certain way, predictions of what will happen when you press that button or engage that feature.

Our brains tell stories to help us understand what's happening around us and how to respond. In the simplest terms, our brains identify the cause-and-effect relationship between two or more things.

> Our brains tell stories to help us understand what's happening around us and how to respond.

This is what we mean when we say neurons make narratives. After all, that's what a story is: a sequence of events that communicates meaning. In essence, your thoughts are the story the Narrator is telling you about your circumstances. And the Narrator never rests. Your brain is creating these little stories nonstop.

Identifying the Narrator

In the 1960s neuroscientist Michael Gazzaniga began studying patients with a fascinating brain condition. One case in particular helps us see how powerful our subconscious need to explain events is.

A young man, called P.S. in the literature, had undergone a procedure to sever his corpus callosum, the dense web of nerves joining the right and left sides of the brain. The procedure, pioneered in 1962, sounds barbaric today but offered relief in extreme cases of brain injury or disease. It also produced a rare opportunity for researchers to learn about the brain's two hemispheres.

Most people know the two hemispheres perform different functions. Though it's not as simple as the old trope we've all heard—*the left side is logical and the right creative*—the left hemisphere does excel at recognizing previously learned patterns, while the right specializes in identifying unique features.[10] And since language is a previously learned pattern, the left side handles most elements of speech. That's important in the case of P.S. and what Gazzaniga discovered.

Once surgeons severed the corpus callosum, the two sides of the brain could no longer communicate with each other. The sides would go on working, but they would be unable to share information. As the saying goes, "The right hand wouldn't know what the left was doing," and vice versa.

After the operation, Gazzaniga and his research partner, Joseph Ledoux, had P.S. focus intently at a dot in the center of a computer screen. By flashing words and images on one side of the dot or the other, they could effectively conceal the information from the opposite, disconnected side of the brain.[11]

Using this technique, Gazzaniga and Ledoux showed simple commands to only the right side of P.S.'s brain. In response, P.S. would stand, laugh, wave, or whatever he was instructed to do. And then Gazzaniga and Ledoux asked why he'd acted that way.

Since the left side of P.S.'s brain didn't realize he'd received any instructions, the most accurate answer would have been something like "I don't know." But here's what's wild: P.S.'s left hemisphere cooked up invented reasons instead. Ledoux explained,

When the command to the right hemisphere was "stand," P.S. would explain his action by saying he needed to stretch. When it was "wave," he said he thought he saw a friend. When it was "laugh," he said we were funny.[12]

None of these answers were true. They were convenient—and basically automatic—fictions to explain personal experience.

Thanks to the severed communication, the left hemisphere had no idea what was going on. But, says Gazzaniga, "It would not be satisfied to state it did not know. It would guess, prevaricate, rationalize, and look for cause and effect, but it would always come up with an answer that fit the circumstances."

Gazzaniga has studied other patients with similar results. The left hemisphere has a need to explain and doesn't mind making stuff up to do it. Gazzaniga says this finding is "the most stunning result from split-brain research," especially when we realize it applies to healthy brains too.[13]

"This is what our brain does all day long," he says. "It takes input from various areas of our brain and from the environment and synthesizes it into a story that makes sense."[14]

The difference is that in the brains of healthy people the two hemispheres can still communicate, so the stories are more reliable. But the impulse is identical.

When we ask why something happened or why things are the way they are, we're acting on a biologically driven, neurologically wired need to understand what's happening around us. Otherwise, our experiences would seem random, leaving us with no way of knowing how to navigate through life.

That's the Narrator. Its job is to interpret all the raw data of experience and offer it back to us in a way that connects the dots. It provides the explanatory glue that holds it all together.[15] And it's got a mind of its own.

Working behind the Scenes

Our brain accounts for only about 2 percent of our body mass. Yet it consumes about 20 percent of our oxygen supply every day.[16] What's our brain up to that requires so much energy? Mostly keeping us alive.

Our body has autonomic processes running all the time— breathing, pumping blood, maintaining balance, and many others. These are done unconsciously. We usually notice them only when there's a problem. But the brain is also busy under the radar cataloging and linking concepts.

We're capable of having only one conscious thought at a time.[17] The thoughts we're aware of thinking represent just a fraction of the work our brain does without our notice.

All day and night, the various regions of the brain are in constant communication. They process information from our senses, sorting and consolidating memory, puzzling on problems, and telling stories.

There are competing theories of how this works. One popular theory suggests that conscious thought is the moment when information from outside (or inside) the brain becomes important or salient enough for us to pay extra attention.

This has sometimes been referred to as daemons in the mind. All the little daemons, which correlate to the various regions and subregions of the brain, chatter in a flurry of subconscious cross talk.[18]

But let's say something affecting our safety or curiosity hits our senses. Suddenly the cross talk converges and gets loud enough that we start paying attention. The daemons bounce the idea up to our conscious mind.

Researchers have actually isolated this *aha* moment while conducting brain scans. It's indicated by a spike of what are called P3 waves.[19] If the cross talk gets loud enough or comes from enough regions of the brain, a P3 wave appears.

That's the moment we become aware of something, and that means we become conscious of things *after* they happen. As neuroscientist Stanislas Dehaene says, "Consciousness lags behind the world."[20]

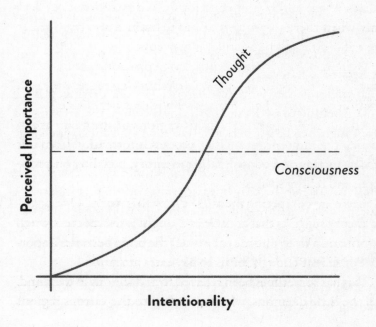

THE UNCONSCIOUS is constantly preloading your conscious mind with thoughts and emotions. We don't know how we thought of them. They're just there. It's like we're always running late to a meeting, and the unconscious mind helps us by stuffing a file folder with information and passing it to us as we enter the boardroom.

The contents of the folder are the raw materials the Narrator is working with. And that's why many of our stories about the world appear to be self-evident, true, and infallible. They're just stories, but our brain presents them as if they're solid facts.

I feel anxiety and tremble when I stand in front of an audience, so speaking must be dangerous.

I don't have what it takes to succeed in this situation, so there's no sense in trying.

I can't see my way past this obstacle to my goal, so it must be impossible.

Thoughts like these guide our actions thousands of times a day, from the mundane to the major. The Narrator tells us what to do when we're bored, distracted, elated, angry, sad, frustrated, whatever.

It's talking when we're reading social media, driving, playing golf, listening to podcasts, analyzing a contract, exercising, or deciding when to get married, start a new business, or change neighborhoods.

Whatever results we're shooting for in life, the Narrator is present—usually helping but sometimes hurting. The Narrator doesn't always get it right. Sometimes it's working against us.

The Narrator's Ungainly Leap

By storing and recalling concepts, we get a sense of what's happening in the world around us, what it means for us in the

That's why many of our stories about the world appear to be self-evident, true, and infallible. They're just stories, but our brain presents them as if they're solid facts.

moment, and what we need to do to plan and act successfully. This is how and why we form memories and imagine the future.[21] And this forward-looking nature of our thoughts is essential for understanding the Narrator.

The Narrator's job is to gather all the spotty data we pick up with our senses or learn from other people and stitch it all into some sort of meaningful storyline, something that makes sense of what we know and helps us deal with what we don't know.

This effort involves a mix of subconscious and conscious guesswork, what neuroscientists call *prediction*, basically creating mental models of the world from all of its whirling, swirling signals.[22] And it mostly works. It's how we maintain relationships, hold down jobs, raise kids, and all the other things we do as humans.

But the Narrator makes some ungainly leaps too. Why are sales down? *Must be the economy.* Why did that driver cut in front of me? *She's reckless.* Why did we lose that game? *The refs were incompetent.* Why did you lie to me? *You must be trying to cheat me.* Why is this happening to me? *I must have done something to deserve it.*

Maybe. Then again, maybe not. The Narrator is a master at labeling problems and recommending solutions. But we shouldn't always take its interpretations for granted. Especially when they interfere with achieving our goals. We've already encountered several examples of that in this chapter:

I'm not a gifted speaker.
Sharing with a group is dangerous.
There must be something wrong with me.

When the Narrator feeds us lines like these, we need to be ready to challenge it. But before we learn how to do that, let's get a better understanding of how our brain shapes the stories it tells.

THREE

How Your Brain Shapes Stories

When I (Michael) told my coach about our financial performance, I didn't think about the fact that my explanation was a story. It's a funny oversight when you remember that I was the CEO of a publishing company: the whole business is stories!

My lack of awareness put me at a disadvantage. Why? Because our stories rest on assumptions and are shaped for specific purposes, and those assumptions and purposes determine how accurate, useful, and empowering our stories will be.

I had all sorts of interesting facts in my story. Gas prices really were up. Same with interest rates. And foot traffic in stores was measurably down, which seemed important because online sales weren't as big as they are today.

Notice how the way I assembled the facts created an air of inevitability: Because prices and interest rates were up, people had less money to spend on books; so, they were not going to bookstores to buy books. What's more, I could (and did) marshal all sorts of official confirmation of my story.

But there were other ways to see the same facts. Maybe people did have less discretionary money—but books are a relatively inexpensive source of entertainment and information. And maybe gas prices were up—but online retailers were still taking orders.

The truth is that my assumptions were a bit iffy. And, it turns out, so was my purpose. Upon reflection, my story was less about explaining reality than it was about ensuring people—like the board to which I reported—knew that my team and I were on top of things *despite* missing the plan.

In other words, it was PR. And as my coach pointed out, it was also a trap. Strategies that might have improved our performance in July could also help us hit our numbers in August. But because my story was more about looking good than performing better, it ensured we'd never get creative and identify those strategies.

My assumptions and the purpose toward which I was striving formed a story about our past results that did not factor in any personal responsibility, which had a direct and negative bearing on our strategies in the present. The story insulated us from blame. It also inadvertently denied us our own agency and the impetus for improvement.

Thank God my coach noticed what I was doing and called me on it. It remains one of the most important lessons I ever learned in business.

MY OWN (MEGAN'S) STORY of avoiding the stage high-lights the same dynamic. Based on my physical reaction to the thought of speaking—racing heart, spiking adrenaline—I assumed speaking was dangerous.

This assumption was confirmed by situations such as when my friend came undone when speaking to our class. And the impression was cemented every time I thought about speaking. My heart would start pounding and my neck would flush red at the prospect of speaking up. So I didn't.

Based on that assumption, my overriding purpose became staying safe and avoiding harm. I limited myself and put a lid on my potential at work and in other areas. And just like in my dad's story, my assumptions were a trap.

Our assumptions and purposes drive our stories, which de-termines our performance. We'll cover purposes in the next chapter. For now, let's dig into assumptions. Where do they come from? It boils down to a simple formulation: assumptions are everything you've *earned* by direct experience or *learned* through the input of others.

It Starts with Personal Experience

Most people don't need anyone to tell them to avoid touching a hot stove a second time. Your brain is more than capable of making that connection on its own. The sequence goes some-thing like this:

$$stove = heat$$
$$heat = burn$$
$$burn = pain$$
$$pain = \textit{watch out!}$$

So we pay more attention around hot stoves. Our experiences are marvelous meaning makers, especially when they are strongly positive or negative.

All our stories are rooted in experience and stored in our memory. When we recall those memories, it can feel as though we're reliving them.

We know a lot about the way memory works thanks to another famous patient known in the research literature by his initials. After a decade of terrible seizures following an accident, H. M. underwent an experimental procedure in 1953 to remove his hippocampi. We all have two of these structures, one in each hemisphere of the brain just below our temples; curiously, they look a bit like a seahorse, which is where the name *hippocampus* comes from.

The removal procedure put a stop to H. M.'s seizures. But it also stopped his memory from working properly. It turns out the hippocampus is essential for incorporating new experiences into our memories.

Thanks to research following this discovery, scientists now think the hippocampus indexes neural patterns and serves them up for our neocortex to use as needed. The interaction of these two distinct parts of the brain allows our mind to reassemble—to re-member—neural patterns forged during an original experience, calling those ideas back to mind more or less as we first experienced them.[1]

Researchers can see this happen in the brain. Functional magnetic resonance imaging (fMRI) shows patterns of neural activity formed during a task and how they were recreated and rehearsed in the hippocampus after the task was complete. "It is as if the brain keeps rewinding a movie scene until it can recite it by heart," said one writer describing the findings.[2]

The Narrator develops stories as the brain retraces its steps. And that's what happens with the hippocampus, which is also responsible for spatial navigation.

The storytelling function of the brain uses this feature of the hippocampus to move through remembered or imagined mental spaces—sequences of people, things, and other concepts that populate our narratives.[3]

Two Kinds of Memory

The hippocampus facilitates two kinds of memory: *episodic* and *semantic*. Episodic memory records our memory of events that involved us. It enables us to move through our mental space, not only recalling prior experiences, but also imagining future scenarios, something we'll cover in greater detail in the next chapter.

Semantic memory is all about facts, data, objects, and events that don't involve us but which we find significant enough to retain.[4] It's knowing the facts to pass chemistry, the voting record of your congressperson, what the blinking signals on a car mean, or that *i* comes before *e* except after *c*.

One quick and dirty distinction is that episodic memory is subjective and semantic is objective. But here's what's curious: The more we replay episodic memory in our minds, the more objective it can feel. This is why the rush of adrenaline when being asked to speak onstage seems to spell certain danger; a subjective experience now feels like an objective fact, even though it's really not.[5]

Information that begins as subjective (our experience) can take on the air of objective truth (reality itself).

It's why we remember the playground slide from our childhood as being monstrously tall, even though it was only six feet in height. That's the way we experience it in our memory. Whatever we recall about the past seems absolutely, objectively true even when it's factually inaccurate.

Information that begins as subjective (our experience) can take on the air of objective truth (reality itself).

None of us are purely neutral observers. Our memories are selective and shaded by our biases and emotions. Memoirists seem to get this more readily than the rest of us. The intentional act of retrieving and retelling memories reveals how wobbly our recollections can be.

"I'm sure I have placed some events in the wrong years or have written that something happened at one place when it happened in another," says author Frank Schaeffer at the start of one of his memoirs, adding the caveat: "What I've written comes from a memory deformed by time, prejudice, flawed recall, and emotion."[6]

Those distortions of our memory shape the stories we tell about ourselves, other people, and the world. "The facts are never just coming at you but are incorporated by an imagination that is formed by your previous experience," says novelist Philip Roth in his memoir *The Facts*. "Memories of the past are not memories of facts but memories of your imaginings of the facts."[7]

We are likely to be overinfluenced by positive experiences and unduly prejudiced by negative ones. As has been so often stated, we remember the past better than it really was. And sometimes worse. Better or worse, we often remember it differently than it was.

Shaped by What Others Think

Another key influence on our assumptions is our network of relationships. This network includes not only the people we directly know, but the wider community of people we live with. It's our cliques, our workplaces, our neighborhood, our city, our country, our society, even our history.

Think about the million things we don't know. Maybe it's how toilets and telephones operate, how birds and butterflies migrate, how skyscrapers and airplanes stay up, whatever. Ignorance is infinite. There's just too much to know and not enough time, attention, or mental capacity to learn it all.

So we rely on what others tell us. In fact, most of the thoughts we think were given to us by others. "Human beings begin to receive, as soon as they can learn to understand, reports, reports of reports, reports of reports of reports," say S. I. Hayakawa and Alan Hayakawa in their book *Language in Thought and Action*.[8] And those reports are full of *whats* and *whys*, facts and explanations, some of which are faulty.

While keeping some ideas and rejecting others, our Narrator incorporates all the pass-along ideas into stories. And usually we do this without much conscious awareness. This comes in handy on the job, navigating a first date, or impressing friends on trivia night.

All of us are the product of a community, and that community exerts a great influence on our thinking. "Whatever we think we know, whether we're right or wrong, arises from our interactions with other human beings," says Baylor University professor Alan Jacobs. "Thinking independently, solitarily, 'for ourselves,' is not an option."[9]

Sometimes the stories our community contributes are helpful. For example, many of us gained our work ethic, moral values, and basic lifestyle practices from our families. Their stories about the value of hard work, integrity, and healthful living served them well and may continue to help you navigate the world. Other stories may be unhelpful.

A popular line attributed to motivational speaker Jim Rohn states that you're the average of the five people you spend the most time with. That rings true but doesn't go nearly far enough. In reality, your thoughts, beliefs, behaviors, and even well-being are influenced by a vast network of friends, family, and acquaintances.

RESEARCHERS Nicholas Christakis and James Fowler made this discovery during a long-term study of heart patients. Everything from obesity to tobacco use and happiness demonstrates network effects. Friends—and friends of friends—impact our own habits and health.[10] Even having friends who have happy friends makes you 6 percent more likely to be happy yourself, according to one study.[11]

The influence of the people around you is far more powerful than most realize. "To dwell habitually with people," says Jacobs, "is inevitably to adopt their way of approaching the world, which is a matter not just of ideas but also of practices."[12]

The fifth-grade teacher who said you were good at math was providing a story for you. So was the teenage boy who thought you were cute, and your crush's father who said you were reckless. Your religious tradition provides stories about the origin of life and its meaning. Your biology professor, favorite singer, or best friend may provide another version of those stories.

We usually add these stories to our mental library without much question. We believe what our parents tell us. We trust the judgment of our friends. We may even believe the negative stories told by people who dislike us. In each case, we're trying to find the meaning behind what we experience, and we use the information gleaned from others to fill in the gaps.

"We live in a community of knowledge," as cognitive scientists Steven Sloman and Philip Fernbach say.[13] Our stories about the world are heavily influenced by or received from the people around us. And, whether earned by direct experience or learned by others, our Narrator's stories come with a built-in tendency toward confirmation.

Why It Feels Great to Be Right

Why did I (Michael) feel so confident in the story I told my coach? Probably for the same reason we conclude that the marketing campaign "will never work" and then it breaks all previous records, or that we're the best employee in the department—just before we're fired.

Our stories are generally consistent with our experience and with the world as we have known it up to now. They make sense to us. They seem true and reliable—right up until we realize they're not.

You've probably seen the results of this dozens of times in business, politics, relationships, personal health, and other contexts. We try the same strategies over and over with marginal—or no—success because we're sure of our stories, even though the results say otherwise.

We like to be right and it's easy to convince ourselves we are. The Narrator harnesses the brain's reward circuitry to reinforce stories. When faced with novel ideas or experiences, we try to explain them by diving into our libraries of stories: our episodic and semantic memories.

When we find something that seems similar or otherwise relevant, we try to explain the new thing in terms of the old. And finding a match triggers a reward: we get a dopamine hit. "The pleasurable feeling that our explanation is the right one—ranging from a modest sense of familiarity to the powerful and sublime 'a-ha!'—is meted out by the same reward system in the brain integral to drug, alcohol, and gambling addictions," says neurologist Robert Burton.[14]

Our assumptions tend to reinforce themselves. The more times we make these explanatory connections, the more certain they feel. As Burton explains, this goes back to an idea called Hebb's Law. You've probably heard it before: "Neurons that fire together wire together."

As our Narrator floats old stories to explain new situations, this reinforces synaptic connections. That's where we get default answers, knee-jerk explanations, and other handy scripts. We've hardcoded them into our neural network.

And to the extent our stories are accurate—or at least advantageous—that's a good thing. It helps us move quickly and confidently through the world, because most of the things we believe are at least true enough to help us make good decisions.

But there's a funny downside to being right nearly all the time. It's hard to see, let alone admit, when our thinking is off. When our thoughts are usually so reliable, it's tough to see when they're steering us in the wrong direction.

Unwinding Unhelpful Stories

In my (Megan's) case, it took years to unwind the story my Narrator spun for me. Life was conspiring to help me challenge my story about public speaking. For one thing, my job kept demanding it. Little by little I had to step up to the mic, literally and figuratively.

My confidence grew as I spoke at a distance (video and podcasts) or with other people (onstage panels and Q&As). But I mostly hated it and how it made me feel. Sometimes it was my personal version of hell.

It was everything I could do sometimes not to burst into tears and run out of our recordings. And the thought of speaking alone onstage still felt life-threatening. But it also felt inevitable, like I couldn't run from it. That was just another story, of course, but it felt every bit as true as the belief that speaking would kill me.

My two stories collided at American Airlines in Chicago's O'Hare Airport on June 16, 2018. I couldn't stop the tears, because I had just pressed Send on the most vulnerable text message of my entire life. I admitted a humiliating and debilitating fear to my friend Michele, who happens to be a dynamite speaking coach.

I knew that if I didn't choose to overcome that fear and step into what my destiny and my calling were becoming, my life was going to get smaller and smaller. I knew that I would have to say no to more and more opportunities. That became untenable to me.

"Hi, Michele," I started. "I'm sitting at the airport in Chicago headed home, and I have something I need to talk to you about, because I'm pretty sure you're the expert. I need to speak publicly, but I have a secret: I'm scared out of my mind."

"But the time has come. I need help to conquer this fear without falling flat on my face and making it even worse. Do you think we could talk sometime? I think you might have some ideas. Thanks for listening. I've never told anybody about this fear other than Joel. Honestly, it's a dam-breaking kind of moment for me."

Tears ran down my face as I sent that message. I sat there crying and realized that until that moment, I had hidden my fear because I was so ashamed of how much fear I felt. After all, I was a successful executive running a high-growth company all about performance coaching, yet in this area I couldn't perform or coach myself.

And I was sick and tired of living that way. I had no idea how I was going to face my fear, but I knew I had to do it. There was no turning back, even if I wanted to. My team wouldn't let me.

They didn't know about the knots my Narrator had tied me into. But they did know they wanted me to speak. Shortly after I sent that note to Michele, my team came up with the crazy idea of hosting a thousand-attendee event, called Achieve, in just three months. And they wanted me to keynote.

WHETHER IT'S SOMETHING EARNED or learned, our assumptions have limitations. When we assume the world is exactly like whatever we've thought, seen, done, encountered, felt, tasted, or touched, we've limited our data sample to exactly one. And—to state the obvious—we don't know everything.

Our stories are limited by the existing neural connections of our brains.[15] Anything we know based solely on our experience will be limited by that same experience. Anything we know

Anything we know based solely on our experience will be limited by that same experience. Anything we know based on the reports of others' experiences will be limited by their limitations and ours combined.

based on the reports of others' experiences will be limited by their limitations and ours combined.

Our thoughts run along familiar paths we've used before. And why not? They're usually right, or at least accurate enough to produce decent—sometimes amazing—results. But other times our stories aren't working for us at all. And other more empowering stories will possibly produce far better results.

The bad news is that we may never discover those stories unless we challenge our assumptions. As neuroscientist Beau Lotto says, "If you attack a problem with the wrong assumption, there is nowhere to go but deeper into that assumption, whether you know you're getting further from the truth or not."[16]

As we'll see in the next chapter, that's a huge problem. Because our brain tells stories to help us navigate the world and achieve our goals. If we build faulty narratives on questionable assumptions, they'll undermine our results.

FOUR

Your Brain's Big Project

What happens when a mom sees a kid's sock on the floor? How many times had author Jennifer Griffin Graham told her child to pick up after himself? And now, despite all the nagging and instruction, there was another one: a pink-and-white sock strewn on the ground.

But when Graham stooped to pick it up, she realized she'd been duped! Her clever son had photocopied a sock, cut out the image, and placed it on the floor to trick his mom.

"My kid discovered you can photocopy anything," she said, "and now he's trying to prank me." The incident, which Graham originally shared on Twitter, was amusing enough it got picked up by the news.[1]

Is it a sock? Sure. Is it a sock? No. And that's an important lesson when it comes to what the Narrator is trying to help us do. The story reminded us of surrealist painter René Magritte and his 1929 painting "The Treachery of Images." It depicts a pipe with the caption "*Ceci n'est pas une pipe*," French for "This is not a pipe."[2]

It caused quite a stir at the time. You can imagine what people said: *What do you mean it's not a pipe? What else could it be?* Polite society assumed Magritte was questioning basic reality.

But the caption is dead right. A picture of a pipe is not the same thing as a pipe. Yes, it resembles a pipe. But you can't stuff Magritte's picture with tobacco, light it, or smoke it. Just as a photocopied sock is not truly a sock, a painting of a pipe is not a pipe. The same is true of our thoughts. A story about a thing is not the thing. It only represents it.

We've said that our stories are shaped by our assumptions and our purposes. That entails what we want, what we're after, our desires, our goals. The Narrator draws on our memories of the past to help us perform in the present to get what we want in the future.

"At the root of human existence is the question: What's next?" says Beau Lotto.[3] Our ability to survive and thrive depends on how well we answer that question. It's your brain's big project.

With a hundred billion neurons and trillions of synaptic connections, there's virtually no limit to the number of thoughts and emotions we can entertain. But these storylines are shaped not only by assumptions but also by the goals themselves.

We use our cause-and-effect reasoning (chap. 2) along with our memories (chap. 3) to create rich, detailed stories about the world so we know how to move successfully within it. In this chapter we'll explore how those stories come together to help us achieve our goals, and how they sometimes lead us off track.

Mind the Gap

Our minds are geared to think about potentials and actuals. There's (a) what you want to have and (b) what you actually have. There's (a) where you want to be and (b) where you actually are. There's (a) who you want to become next and (b) who you are right now.

The gap between the two states and what we do about it provides the central drama of our lives. It's the action in action movies, the romance in romance novels, and the solving of mysteries in detective stories. Without the gap, nothing happens.

The effort to close the gap is what drives progress in our lives. The central drama of our lives is producing desired results. That's not the sum total of our experience, or the most valuable aspect of our lives, but it is basic to being a living, thinking creature on this planet.

So how do we close the gap? We know from what we've encountered so far that if we're looking to get unstuck or uplevel some area of our life, we need to focus on the stories we're telling ourselves about the obstacles or opportunities we're facing.

Our world is constructed in our minds. Everything we know about the concrete world is mediated through our eyes, ears, nose, and the rest of our senses and processed in the brain. As physicist David Deutsch says, "Reality is out there: objective, physical and independent of what we believe about it. But we never experience that reality directly."[4]

Instead, our brains receive information through our senses, then sort, label, and store it, always searching for connections between what we've experienced in the past, what we're experiencing in the present, and what we anticipate experiencing in the future.[5]

This does not negate the possibility of objective reality outside of us. It's just that our experience of it will be subjective.

Deutsch refers to this function of the brain as a "virtual-reality generator."[6] Neuroscientists sometimes refer to it as simulation. When people say that we are living in a simulation, we laugh and say that it sounds absurd. And it does sound absurd. But it's true in this narrow, technical sense: our brain is creating a simulation of reality that we inhabit.[7]

Most of us are probably more accustomed to thinking in terms of imagination. Whatever we call this capacity of our mind, our Narrator uses it to plan and predict the outcomes of our actions. *If I do x, will it achieve y?*

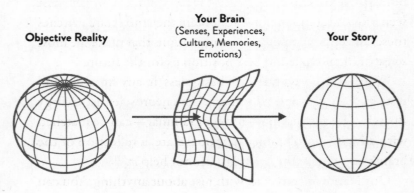

Objective Reality   **Your Brain**   **Your Story**
                          (Senses, Experiences,
                           Culture, Memories,
                              Emotions)

Best-Guess Stories

One of the first people to realize our interlinking neurons were busy simulating reality was the Cambridge psychologist Kenneth Craik. In the 1940s he theorized that our brains modeled reality so we could think about it and decide—consciously or unconsciously—how best to act in it. "The fundamental feature of neural machinery [is] its power to parallel or model external events," he wrote.[8]

Craik's thinking is now standard. The stories we tell are like narrative models of the world in which we can run alternative scenarios in anticipation of future events, all so we can better perform in the event itself.[9]

We are like characters in our own story. And we're drafting and redrafting the next scene in hopes of coming up with the best path to the goal we're pursuing. We have to redraft because so many storylines don't get us what we want. Some are disastrous, and it's better to let our character fail in our minds and then try something else than to fail in the real world.[10]

By connecting and reconnecting the concepts in our personal library of experience, we can try out any number of different scenarios and combinations. Your brain then mixes and matches these concepts, searching for combinations that make the most sense of the present and best position us for the future.

"The brain always takes its 'best guess' in any situation and tests its most plausible hypothesis," says neuroscientist György Buzsáki. "Each situation—novel or familiar—can be matched with a highest probability neuronal state, a reflection of the brain's best guess. The brain just cannot help it."[11]

Our Narrator can work with just about anything. You can hear it in the way we talk about new challenges or opportunities.

"It's like x or y," we say, hunting for a link to something we already know that will shed light on z. If we can find a link, however tenuous, we will—and usually do.

"There is no such thing as unknown for the brain," says Buzsáki. "Every new mountain, river, or situation has elements of familiarity, reflecting previous experiences in similar situations, which can activate one of the pre-existing original trajectories."[12]

Our relative success in the future depends on how advantageously our best-guess stories, based on the past, map to present realities. But it's important to stress that, like the photocopied sock or the painted pipe, our stories are only representations.

The stories we tell about reality resemble reality, but they are not reality. They are the Narrator's attempt to represent reality to us. Another way of saying this is that stories are not facts by themselves. They are facts plus our interpretations and causal links.

Remember what Judea Pearl said in chapter 2: The world is made up of both facts and the "intricate web of cause-effect relationships" we use to make sense of the facts. He also said this causal glue, not the simple facts, comprises most of what we know.[13]

Our knowledge is a mix of fact and fancy, and there's nothing wrong with that. In fact, there are tremendous upsides. For instance, that distinction leaves room for imagination and everything it entails. The problems enter when we mistake our opinions and hunches for reality.

MOST OF THE TIME, our brains do a decent job of representing reality. The brain is capable of painting a pretty solid picture of a tree, for example, or a car, or a person. But as the situation gets more complex, the brain relies more and more heavily on guesswork. That is to say, our brain fills in gaps of what the senses don't pick up directly.[14]

Based on everything we've earned and learned, we make decisions about what to do next. And we think we understand what's happening in our own thoughts or the world around us because our brain has provided a plausible storyline—a prediction. But once in a while, our brain gets the prediction wrong. That usually happens when something about the circumstances has changed.

Think about driving. As you look out your windshield and glance from one mirror to another, you think you're seeing everything around you. What's actually happening is that your brain takes a series of pictures through eye movements known as saccades, then stitches them together for you, filling in the blanks based on the context.

That explains why you can look both ways at a stop sign and still not see the approaching motorcycle. It's small enough to fit between the images your brain has captured. Your brain sees what it expects to see. It's best-guessing.

Sometimes that happens when you received the story from someone else who was simply mistaken. Your mother told you to go to grad school because you'd be sure to get a great job. Your best friend told you to move to Nashville because that's how you land a record deal. Your first employer told you that the customer is always right. But they're not, actually.

Other ideas are based on predictions that were once highly reliable. Take walking down a sidewalk, for example. Most of the time you do this without conscious thought. Your brain remembers the length of your stride, the height of your shoe heel, the speed you're going. Based on that experience, it predicts the next step. You don't even have to look at your feet. Your brain tells your foot precisely where to land next based on experience. End of story.

But once in a while, your brain gets the prediction wrong. That usually happens when something about the context has changed. You got new shoes with a slightly higher heel. There's a crack in the sidewalk that wasn't there before. It's raining and the surface is wet. If you're deep in thought or in a hurry, your brain may not have time to factor in this new information. So you trip. The context changed and that made the story unreliable.

The ancient philosopher Heraclitus said, "You can never step into the same river twice." Though it may appear unchanged, the water that flowed yesterday is long gone this morning. When we are unwilling to revise our thinking in light of changing circumstances, we wind up with an unreliable story.

What you see, or think you see, or know, or think you know, is not always accurate. And this is where our stories can break down.

> When we are unwilling to revise our thinking in light of changing circumstances, we wind up with an unreliable story.

Our perceptions are imperfect, which is why eyewitnesses will often present different accounts of the same incident.

If we're honest, these prediction errors—while usually not disastrous—happen frequently. Your mind makes a correlation between two concepts, but gets the meaning wrong.

Your Narrator has gathered what your senses tell you, filtered it through your experience, community, and imagination, and presented you with a story you swear was about a

sock or a pipe. But it's not. It's a best-guess photocopy or a painting made by your brain.

When it comes to mundane experiences like locating your car keys or crossing the street, your brain represents reality quite well. When trying to interpret more complex situations, the brain can come up with an interpretation of the facts that is disastrously wrong. Consider what happens when we try to guess what others are thinking.

Mind Reading for Fun and Profit

Though no one can literally read minds, we can often make a pretty good guess at another person's thoughts based on subtle clues such as facial expression, body language, tone of voice, and other signs. Coupled with our own library of experiences and explanations, we can get a good sense of what other people are thinking.

Psychologists call this ability to imagine what others are thinking *theory of mind*, and even babies are surprisingly good at it. They have an innate ability to guess the mental states, moods, and even intentions of other people.

We do the same thing when we determine that a family member or coworker is upset based on their choice of words or even their silence. We may intuit that someone is untrustworthy based on clues we're barely aware of, such as eye movement or the disconnect between their smiling lips and passionless eyes.

We also use this ability in far more complex situations, such as making deals and negotiating contracts, selling a boss on a project idea, launching products in a new market, offering advice, or leading a team. We're constantly making guesses about what other people are thinking—and what others might think about what others think.

We can extend that thinking through several degrees of social separation because the neural networks in our brains are extremely complex. In fact, scientists have discovered a link between the size of a mammal's neocortex as a percentage of total brain size and the size of that animal's social group.[15] Our brains are practically designed for this kind of complex, speculative thought in a social context.

The fact that you got married or entered a relationship, landed a job, closed the sale on a house, negotiated a raise, or any other complex social interaction shows that your imagination as it relates to theory of mind functions reasonably well. That's enormously helpful in navigating through life.

It is "the glue of social interactions," according to neuropsychologist Elkhonon Goldberg. "Individuals that are deficient in the 'theory of mind' department are at a huge social disadvantage."[16] We might say they have poor social skills. It would be just as accurate to say that they lack imagination. It's an amazingly useful skill. In fact, some scholars think our ability to imagine the mental states of others is fundamental to our ability to think about our own mental state. When we ask, "What do I think about such and such?" we're essentially treating our own mind as an other.[17]

However, our thoughts about other people's thoughts are always guesses. In more complex situations, they are guesses layered upon guesses. We're guessing what other people think based on what we think they think about what still others are thinking, and so on. With all that speculation, there's a reasonable chance of getting the story wrong.

COMPLICATING THE MATTER further is the fact that we're basically programmed to find the *why*. When we don't know what other people are thinking, we have to cook up a reason. So we usually make some sort of guess, and sometimes we're wildly off base.

He said that because she wants me off this project.
She's talking to me a lot because she thinks I'm interesting.
He's late because he doesn't respect my time.
She's trying to run me off the road!

We can speculate on the thoughts and intentions of others, but that's different from knowing. Our stories are based on reality. They are not reality itself. This means they are liable to error. Some come from our experience and are restricted by our experience. Others are influenced by or received from others, so they are limited by the bounds of our social network. And some we just make up.

That doesn't mean our stories are wrong. It does mean that they are no more accurate than our impressions, which are always subjective. When our predictions fail us—"Wow, that last step was a doozy"—our brain usually adapts pretty quickly.

It goes back to the concept library and makes different connections, looking for a combination of concepts that's more useful.[18] That's especially important when we're fixated on a goal.

Goals Create the Plotline

Seventeen-year-old Hugh Herr was something of a prodigy in the rock-climbing world. By age eight, he'd climbed all 11,627 feet of Mount Temple in southern Alberta, Canada. As a teen, he'd scaled an especially difficult approach to Shawangunk Ridge, near Albany, New York, on his first try—something no one had done before.

Then in January 1982, Herr set out to climb Mount Washington, the tallest peak in New Hampshire's White Mountains. But the trip turned disastrous.

Caught in a freak blizzard, he became lost on the descent and nearly died. Frostbite destroyed his legs. Attempts to save his limbs failed, and surgeons amputated both legs just below the knee. "You'll never be able to climb those mountains again," Herr's doctor told him.[19]

How do you think Herr responded?

Before we answer, remember that our stories reflect not only our past experience but also our future goals. The question "What's next?" is never asked in a vacuum. We have an end in mind and we're searching for the best way to achieve it.

We never think of all possible next actions we might take. There are far too many possible answers to the what's-next question. So our Narrator solves this problem by creating a plot, telling us stories in terms of the goals we're after. But this creates an inevitable outcome. Our brain tells us stories to attain goals, and those goals in turn shape the stories our brain tells.

The doctor's story contained assumptions about what double amputees were capable of, and those assumptions were based on years of experience. Beyond that, his goal was to help his patient adjust to what he assumed was his new reality. Unsurprisingly, the doctor's story was that Herr would never climb again.

But Herr didn't accept the verdict. To return to the idea that launched our chapter, Herr suspected the sock was photocopied, that the pipe was paint. "I dreamed of returning to my chosen sport of mountain climbing," he recounted years later.[20]

That was his goal. But climbing mountains without legs? Impossible as it might seem to his doctor—and probably to most of us—Herr was working with a different set of assumptions. Based on his own experience, Herr realized he didn't need legs, only a means to grip and scale the rock.

His thought process, captured by biographer Alison Osius, is eye-opening:

> "I've lost my legs, not my mind," Hugh thought. "I still have the knowledge and mind-set of a hard rock climber. I still know how to position my body on hard rock walls. I need devices, I need mechanical contrivances that will allow me to connect my physical world with everything I can conceive of doing. . . . I am not handicapped," he thought, "the prosthetic technology is."[21]

Herr's Narrator was clearly working with different materials than the doctor's Narrator was. Determined to climb, Herr went to the machine shop and built himself special prostheses for scaling vertical walls of ice and stone. And a few months later, he set out for the mountains.

Different assumptions and different goals added up to a different story. And that led to a different strategy and better results. Not only was Herr able to climb again, but he could also climb higher and faster than before.

His metal legs didn't get cold or sore, and the "feet" he'd designed fit better into small crevices in the rock. He was also more than ten pounds lighter. A year after his accident, in the spring of 1983, Herr's improbable comeback landed him on the cover of *Outside* magazine.[22]

IF HUGH HERR really could climb mountains, why did his medical team think it impossible? Was he just stronger, bolder, or more courageous than those who treated him? Probably not. But he did have different goals and wasn't hemmed in by the same assumptions.

Faced with a seemingly impossible situation, Herr was willing to question the commonsense response that double amputees cannot climb rock. Instead, he asked, *What would it take?*

Herr's story is a lesson on a critical truth: sometimes our goals enable us to imagine better, more empowering stories. When we commit to an outcome, we can recombine the ideas at our disposal to fashion stories that serve the goal.

We do this all the time but perhaps not as intentionally as we might. Almost nothing works quite the way we imagine. We adjust. Sometimes that adjustment requires rethinking the problem. Depending on the story we tell ourselves about reality, we can create a different reality.

Depending on the story
we tell ourselves about
reality, we can create
a different reality.

Creating a Different Reality

Our brain creates connections every day, forming stories that give meaning to our experience. We use these stories to navigate through every activity from picking a lunch spot ("Their tacos are the best around") to negotiating with a client ("Go for the close, she's ready to buy") and predicting whether we'll like a movie ("This director never disappoints").

Most of the time, our thoughts interpret reality pretty well. If you're reading this book, we bet you've got a fairly accurate understanding of your particular corner of the world and what it takes to be successful in it.

But not always. Every so often we encounter situations in which our stories don't work the way they should. Our brain finds those tacos unappealing. Despite our expectation, the client might go cold and stop responding to emails. And every director has at least one dud.

The Narrator can be a helpful guide, but it's not always right. We think the sock on the floor is really a sock—and then, worse, yell at our child. We think the painting is really a pipe and light it on fire. What happens then?

Our ability to recover from these kinds of mistakes and achieve better results in the future depends entirely on our willingness to revisit our understanding of the situation to make it more complete, accurate, and helpful. We have to interrogate the Narrator, which is the next step in our three-step process.

The good news is that we're not stuck with our stories, even stories we've believed for years and years. We learn and grow as our assumptions are tested in the real world. Then we can gain a clearer picture of reality, learn to tell better stories, and achieve results for ourselves that we'd previously only dared to imagine.

The capacity to imagine a wide range of stories largely sets the bounds of our experience. Why? Because the stories at our disposal drive the strategies we use to pursue our goals. The ability to imagine a better state of affairs is what drives human progress, achievement, and flourishing. And the ability to reimagine our stories when we're stuck or stalled is what enables us to improve our lives, become more productive at work, take control of our health, become better spouses, friends, parents, and more.

This imagination is the product of the stories our Narrator is weaving with the neurons in our brains. And it's the difference between climbing mountains and lowering our expectations.

Herr's doctor couldn't imagine his patient climbing again. But Herr could, and so he did. Climbing onstage to deliver a keynote is not as impressive as climbing a rock face without legs, but that stage was my (Megan's) hill to conquer. And I did.

I'll share more details about the process later, but let me say now that my friend Michele not only answered my text, she responded with an offer to help. If you know Michele, you wouldn't be surprised by that. She's relentlessly gracious and helpful.

But if you know Michele's story, you might also be aware that she had her own mountain to conquer. And it's the perfect story to explain what we need to do to interrogate the Narrator when he leads us astray. We start that process in the next section.

ACTION

Go back to the problem or opportunity you described earlier on your Full Focus Self-Coacher (fullfocus.co/self-coacher). Now describe the story you're telling yourself about it?

WHAT WE KNOW SO FAR

▶ Neurons make narratives—and our narratives determine how successful we are in achieving our goals.

▶ Our Narrator's job is to interpret all the raw data of experience and offer it back to us in a way that connects the dots.

▶ We know loads of facts, but a lot of what we know is not factual but rather the causal inferences that explain how all those facts fit together.

▶ Anything we know based solely on our experience will be limited by that same experience.

▶ Anything we know based on the reports of others' experiences will be limited by their limitations and ours combined.

▶ Our knowledge is a mix of fact and fancy. The problems enter when we mistake our opinions and hunches for reality.

▶ Depending on the story we tell ourselves about reality, we can create a different reality.

▶ The ability to reimagine our stories when we're stuck or stalled is what enables us to get better results and improve our lives.

PART 2

INTERROGATE

CHALLENGE YOUR NARRATOR

FIVE

Separating Fact from Fiction

Our friend Michele Cushatt began her career as a registered nurse but developed a passion for public speaking. With her bright, cheerful voice, charismatic personality, and flawless delivery, she soon became an in-demand motivational and inspirational speaker. In fact, Michele gained such skill and reputation as a communicator that she developed a second career as a speaking coach.

Her clients included A-list celebrities, sports figures, and musicians. For ten years she was at the top of her game, coaching clients who spoke on national stages to huge audiences. Meanwhile, her own speaking platform continued to increase through live events, podcasts, and television.

Then, nearly overnight, her voice was gone.

Michele was treated for squamous cell carcinoma of the tongue three times over five years, which included the removal of more than two-thirds of her tongue, as well as multiple skin, tissue, and vascular grafts. She was unable to make a sound for over a month.

When her voice did return, it had changed dramatically. Her melodic soprano had become a raspy alto. The new shape of her reconstructed tongue produced a slight slurring of her speech. When she tentatively made a return to cohosting a podcast with me (Michael), listener comments were negative to the point of being rude.

"People said the most awful things," Michele recalled. "'I can't listen anymore, it's too painful,' or 'Why don't you go to the dentist and get your dentures fixed?' or 'You should get a speech coach.'" Some suggested she might have a mental disability.

"That's when it hit me," said Michele. "My whole life story has changed. I thought of myself as an expert in my field. I thought I knew what made for good communication. I also knew that I would never again have the warm, powerful vocal quality that made me a great speaker."

That realization began a year of questioning:

Who am I?

Do I need to change careers?

Can I earn a living as a speaking coach, a consultant, or a speaker?

"Those questions, along with the physical loss and the emotional and physical energy that went into sorting this out, were just extraordinary," she said.

WHEN OUR STORIES about who we are or what the world is like no longer match reality, the results can be devastating. Our thoughts are helpful when they serve our purposes—when they help us navigate life. Our success, indeed our survival, depends on how well our stories correspond to the reality we face.

That's tricky, because none of our stories are 100 percent accurate. As we've seen, we automatically form stories, mostly unconsciously. And those narratives are shaped by our assumptions and purposes; we don't notice or include details that don't fit the plot.

The Narrator, while usually well intentioned, is not omniscient. It's limited. And sometimes those limitations leave us stranded by the wayside of life or frustrated we can't go further, faster.

When Joel and I (Megan) were looking for ways to help our boys, it took years to get the right answers. Why? Part of the challenge was finding therapies and therapists who could help. But another challenge was unlearning a lot of what we assumed about parenting.

Our strategies weren't working. And that's because our stories were wonky.

Whenever we're stuck or stalled, we need to examine our stories. In this chapter we're going to look at how to interrogate the Narrator. We'll also explore how to test our stories and separate fact from fiction so we can gain a better, more helpful picture of reality.

How? The first step is to establish the facts. Next, we determine if we know how they fit together properly. We need to ensure we haven't missed any important details. And, as an optional step, we might find it helpful to externalize and explain our thinking to others.

But to get started, we have to go back to the garden of Eden.

Just the Facts, Please

If you recall from chapter 2, the cognitive scientist Judea Pearl noticed something funny about the story of Adam and Eve hiding in the garden: God asked *what* questions and the two gave *why* answers. That is, they went beyond the raw data to supply explanations—same as Michael Gazzaniga's split-brain patient P.S.

We're all the same. We can't help it. So the first step in interrogating our stories is clarifying the facts. That starts by separating the *whats* from the *whys*.

Here's the good news: You've already begun that process by writing about your story. By articulating your beliefs about your situation you're using words you can now analyze.

Start by asking: What are the facts of the story? By facts we mean concepts that are verifiably true. We're talking about objective reality, the raw data.

Not everything presented as true is reliable. Writer Mary Karr talked about this with Krista Tippett for the podcast *On Being*. Karr had a wild, traumatic childhood and learned some unhelpful coping strategies as a result. One was alcohol.

When she got sober, she came to rely on a mentor who could help her learn a different way of managing in the world. When Karr would come with something that bothered or frightened her, her mentor would say, "What is your source of information?"

"Ninety-nine percent of the time," said Karr, "it was: 'I thought it up.'"[1] We all do that. Remember, our brain needs to have an answer. When we don't have one, we try to supply it, with or without evidence.

Does this thing exist out there in the world, or is it only in your head? This isn't a question about your sanity. It's about whether you're dealing with facts or merely your own assumptions about the facts.

Not all thoughts are facts. In fact, most of what we know isn't raw data; as Pearl said, a lot of our knowledge is the explanatory glue that holds those bits of data together. We want to pull the glue apart long enough to examine the individual ideas for their factuality.

KNOWLEDGE

Fact	←———→	Opinion
Objective		Subjective
Actual		Predicted
Reality		Theory
Result		Hypothesis
Observable		Imaginary
Event		Interpretation
Confirmed		Conjecture
Certainty		Guess
Verified		Unfounded
Territory		Map

You're looking for things that are objective, actual, real, observable, and certain. We're talking about stuff that really exists and events that actually happened. They're verifiable, and you can confirm it if need be.

As you do this, be aware: plenty of thoughts masquerade as facts. For instance, conjecture. A guess is not a thing. It's your attempt to create meaning around the cause-and-effect relationship between two things.

Emotions are another thing to pull aside. Though they are real to you, emotions do not represent objective reality. Every emotion can be linked to a cause. I'm angry, *because* she was rude to me. I'm happy, *because* it's my birthday.

Emotions are primarily the labels we apply to feelings in our bodies, according to neuroscientist Lisa Feldman Barrett. We can default to interpreting those signals as a negative emotion (say, fear or anxiety). But through observation and awareness, we can also choose to interpret them in other ways (say, excitement or preparedness). The physical sensation is one thing; what it means is another.[2]

An emotion isn't a fact. It's how you feel about a fact. It's an interpretation. A story.

Same with conclusions. They are our judgments about what the facts mean, which make them stories. It's possible that conclusions could be rigorously evaluated and verified as facts: Colonel Mustard, in the library, with the candlestick. But for now we want to focus on the individual details.

Sometimes it's hard to get to the facts, but it's absolutely essential. "The facts are friendly," as psychologist Carl Rogers said.[3] Even when they tell a story you don't want to hear. Without them, you'll accept faulty stories.

You'll often need to question your experience when examining your thoughts. *Did I really see what I thought I saw? How certain am I that this is what she actually said? What's going on right now that could interfere with my perception? Stress? Fatigue? Excitement? Is there any chance I could be mistaken?*

As you consider the facts, be wary of data limitations and confirmation bias. Your job is to separate the relevant facts from the irrelevant. It's tempting to arrange the facts to tell a positive story. Instead, get the facts on the table before assembling your conclusion.

Sketchy Data and Hasty Conclusions

When the Incan grain quinoa came to public attention it was hailed as a kind of miracle food, especially among those with certain dietary ailments, such as celiac disease. Before long, this little-known foodstuff that was consumed mostly by Andean farmers became popular in the wealthy, Western world.

Prices naturally rose with increased demand. Within a few years the price had tripled. What's more, researchers noted a curious decline in consumption among the original consumers, the growers themselves.

When that story broke, the press had a field day. The *Guardian* went so far as to run the accusing headline, "Can vegans stomach the unpalatable truth about quinoa?"[4] The article asserted that it was now cheaper for poor Peruvians and Bolivians to eat "imported junk food" than the very grain that their land produced.

But the rising quinoa prices in Peru and Bolivia was only half the story. As it turned out, many people were enjoying the extra income from their crops and were eating something else for a change. Far from being starved by global consumption, their increased profit had allowed them more choice in their diet.[5]

When we notice a coincidence of concepts, we have to be cautious about labeling one as the cause of the other. "Hidden common causes are the most frequent sources of misinterpretations based on correlational arguments," says György Buzsáki.[6] There may be other factors at work.

Sales of sunglasses and ice cream increase at the same time. But we cannot conclude that one causes the other, especially since drowning deaths and homicide rates increase along with them. One does not cause any of the others, but there is a common factor that correlates to all of them: the weather.

What we don't know about a problem can be just as important as what we do. Our brain is constantly at work connecting the dots of our experience. To make meaning quickly, it fills in blanks and leaves stuff out. We think we know x causes y, but it turns out that $x + a$ causes y.

We may assume our child hates homework because he likes video games. That may be true, but could he also have a learning disability? We think our coworker was selected for promotion because he's the boss's favorite. Possibly, but could it also be that he has higher customer satisfaction scores?

> **Whatever the story in our head, it's important to ask: Can we really know this based on the evidence we have?**

Whatever the story in our head, it's important to ask: Can we really know this based on the evidence we have? This query forces attention on our connections and conclusions. Does a particular story hold water, or is it full of holes?

We never know everything about any concept or problem, and sometimes that gap in understanding is enormous. Journalist Michael Blastland calls this "the hidden half."[7]

Our minds crave certainty, but it's very hard to come by in a world of limited information. We're nearly always working with partial information and making decisions based on probability.

Incomplete Metaphors

We can see the way we operate with only partial information in our usage of a form of expression you may be completely unaware of: metaphors.

Metaphors have great power over your thoughts and actions. They communicate ideas like lightning, quickly equating one thing with another. That's how they work. A metaphor borrows the meaning of one concept to shed light on another. Linking concepts in this way allows us to make leaps of understanding.

This is a valuable ability, and we use it all the time. Try explaining any subject to someone else and notice how many metaphors you use. We did it several times in the paragraph above—*lightning, borrowing, illumination, leaping*.

"We utter about one metaphor for every ten to twenty-five words, or about six metaphors a minute," says author James Geary, reporting on several studies of language use.[8] Metaphors are shortcuts, and our brains love shortcuts. Without this shorthand way of making connections between concepts, we'd probably spend several hours a day explaining reality to ourselves and others.

We need metaphors and the stories they provide. In fact, metaphors can help you understand problems differently and help you creatively come to new conclusions. But they can also ensure that you misunderstand the situation at hand.

Metaphors are also limiting. When we commit to a metaphor, we start to see what's in front of us only through the lens of what works for that metaphor. "This will, in turn, reinforce the power of the metaphor to make experience coherent," write George Lakoff and Mark Johnson in their book *Metaphors We Live By*. "In this sense metaphors can become self-fulfilling prophecies."[9]

If we say x is like y, we may fail to notice that it's more advantageous to see it like z. But we'll only ever see x in terms of y. Y becomes a mental rut that leads to a predictable but unhelpful strategy.

Sometimes a small part of a metaphor really works, but we let it limit us from seeing the full range of what's happening. For example, once we've decided that the assistant principal is "a real bear," we no longer think about how to interact with him. We simply avoid him. Once you've defined Jeff as a "rock," you'll load him up with difficult assignments and fail to see when he's at his breaking point. If Monique is a "sales machine," you'll expect her closing rate to be reliably high, even if there are other factors at play this month that may lead to different outcomes. The little bit you know prevents you from learning the things you don't know but need to know in order to succeed.

When you interrogate a story, it's vital to strip away the metaphors so that you see the concepts clearly. As you examine your thinking, pay close attention to the metaphors you use—positive or negative. State what you mean by the metaphor; that is, why you think it's an apt comparison. Ask, "Is that really true?" Then recast the story without metaphors. That will give you a clearer picture of the story itself.

Language Traps

Relatedly, another part of interrogating and clarifying your story is paying attention to the language you're using. There are about 170,000 words currently in use in the English language. That gives you a lot of discretion in choosing specific words or phrases to communicate a thought.

The words you choose, therefore, have significance. They communicate not only the facts of the case but also the story you have created about them. For instance, the statements "Have a seat," "Won't you please be seated?" "Grab a seat," and "Park it!" all convey the same imperative, yet each tells a different story.

That relationship works both ways. The words we choose also influence our stories. When we use negative, disparaging, or disempowering words, we reinforce the corresponding stories about ourselves and our situation. Therefore, language can shape the stories we tell by either limiting them or freeing them to change.

I (Michael) began to notice that during a particularly busy season of travel. As I was preparing to leave for a speaking engagement, I felt a bit fatigued and was secretly dreading the idea of hopping on another flight. A friend called and asked me where I was going. I said, "San Jose. I have to speak at a convention." Even as I said the words, I noticed the resignation in my voice.

The moment I hung up, it hit me. *I don't* have to *speak. I* get to *speak.* I followed that thought a little further. *I chose this line of work. I chose to accept this invitation. Many people would gladly do this for free—or even pay for the opportunity. Yet they're paying me to come.* Simple, but that two-minute pep talk dramatically changed my attitude.

Disempowering language is an early warning sign of a false story. Pay attention to the words you choose and the emotional tone that drives them. Sometimes it feels like the mouth has a mind of its own. We just say things out of habit. So you have to be intentionally aware. Trace these thoughts back to their source. Interrogate them, then reimagine how you would state a more positive story.

Start small. Begin using "get to" rather than "have to," for instance. This might require some practice and a little persistence. Then notice the difference it makes in your attitude. For starters, it can suddenly make you grateful. Rather than dreading or resenting an activity, you can be thankful for it. And the more gratitude you express, the better you'll feel and perform.

You have the power to affect your mood, your thoughts, and your results simply by choosing more empowering language. Sometimes, though, your language is fine. The problem is that the context for your story has changed.

When the Details Change

The first map of the United States drawn by an American was created by Abel Buell in 1784 (see below). Buell was an engraver, not a cartographer. He had no survey data on which to base his map. Instead, he based his work on other maps. That meant it was twice removed from the real-world shape of the rivers, mountains, and shorelines of the continent.

Not surprisingly, it contained some glaring inaccuracies. It's hazy in this original document, but Connecticut is pictured to the west of Pennsylvania rather than to the east, and the Mich-

igan peninsula slants curiously to the northwest. Yet Buell's map was a great improvement over its predecessors. It included political boundaries for the newly joined States of the Union, and in a day when waterways rather than roads were used for long-distance travel, Buell's map gave a better depiction of the primary bodies of water and their connections to one another.

It worked well enough for a while. Today, though, this map would be useless either for travel or for understanding the geographical boundaries of the states. Things have changed a great deal since 1784.

Like Buell's map, our ideas may be true and useful in one time and place but not another. Like our stories, maps reflect their goal or purpose. A topographical map, a road map, and a weather map present the same territory in a very different manner. Which is correct? That depends on what you're doing.

If you want to know the terrain so you can travel on foot, try the topo map. To get there by car, you'll need the road map. To choose your clothing for the day, the weather map will be best. If you're using a weather map to drive to California, you'll probably wind up thinking it was a lousy map, even though it was perfectly accurate.

As we've seen, it's the same with stories. Our purpose shapes our stories. And that means we can run into problems if our goals no longer align with the stories we're telling ourselves. What's changed in your expectations for your business? Career? Relationships? How does your story need to change, in light of that changed context?

This is especially critical when we seek to use off-the-rack "truths" and "best practices" cooked up in one context and applied to another.

ONCE WE HAVE A WORKABLE IDEA, we normally want
to make it universal and portable. If it worked once, it'll work
again. If it worked here, it'll work there.

This accounts for the popularity of books touting the value
of "principles" or "laws." Usually, they're based on the expertise
of someone who has had great success in business, coaching,
sports, or any other pursuit. They distill their experience to a
list of rules that worked well for them.

Often those principles will apply to others in similar circumstances. But too many changes in the context will invalidate
the rule. That was the case for LEGO, makers of the iconic
children's building blocks.

Generations of kids have grown up playing with LEGO
blocks, including kids in our own family. But by the late 1990s
the business was struggling due to competition from electronic
games. How could LEGO change the story, recapture their core
audience, and turn the business around?

To answer that question, the company hired Poul Plougmann,
a turnaround expert with deep experience in the electronics industry. Hailed as a miracle worker, Plougmann implemented a
bold strategy based on seven "Principles of Innovation."

These principles, which included "Head for blue-ocean mar-
kets" and "Practice disruptive innovation," certainly sounded
good. And they had worked wonders for companies like Procter
& Gamble, Southwest Airlines, and Canon. Plougmann challenged executives to surpass McDonald's and Coca-Cola to
become "the world's strongest brand among families with
children."[10]

The result was a disaster. In the effort to become more innovative, the company abandoned its core customer, children
who like to build things, in pursuit of children who don't.

Fortunately, the company was able to recover from the error and regain strength by refocusing on its core products, embracing customer input into design, and streamlining production.

The LEGO story doesn't prove that the seven principles are wrong, only that they did not do well in the given context. What works in Seattle may not work in Tampa. A story that helps navigate the construction business may be sadly ineffective in a service industry. When we distill our stories into principles, rules, or laws, we should be aware they might not travel well.[11]

Here are some random elements of context that may change from time to time. When they do, your story may be less accurate than before:

- Demographics
- Staffing
- Availability
- Style
- Customer base
- Competitors
- Education
- Life stage
- Location
- Season
- Time of day
- Economic performance
- Birth
- Marriage
- Divorce
- Death
- Election cycles
- Regulations
- Taxation
- Weather
- Health

This list is not exhaustive. We're sure you can imagine other circumstances that might change and then radically alter outcomes. As Blastland says, "Even if we think we know 99% of what's important, we can be 100% wrong about how it turns out."[12] One floating variable can change our results.

Show Your Work

Contrary to popular belief, science is fundamentally subjective. What do we mean? The scientific enterprise relies on the intuitions, hunches, prejudices, and guesses of scientists who have to trust these flimsy parts of thought while they do the hard work of experimentation with no promise of payoff.

Usually, the only reason a scientist would do the painstakingly hard work of gathering experimental data is because they believe something is either true or untrue—so far without ample evidence—and they are determined to demonstrate that.

Yet in other ways, science is very objective. What accounts for the difference?

A scientist working in the lab is operating in the world of subjective thinking in which they deal with more tentative thought processes. They formulate hypotheses, sometimes based on intuition, which may be accurate or not.

But when it comes time to argue it in public, they have to state it in objective terms or it will be rejected by everyone. So there is the private subjective side, and the public objective side.[13]

The problem is that we sometimes get lost in the subjective side—our own thoughts, hunches, hypotheses. When we do, we're liable to make connections that aren't really there. We make logical leaps in the way we connect the dots of our story.

One such error occurs when we allow our goals to shape our stories, as we mentioned in chapter 4. When we are focused on a particular outcome, we may miss key information that would change the story. Researchers call this *cognitive bias*.

An example might be a husband and wife clashing over household budgets. The numbers are the same, but they have

When we are focused
on a particular
outcome, we may miss
key information that
would change the story.

different goals in mind and so disagree on what constitutes "reasonable" spending. The same is true in business, politics, or any other context. We may look at the same set of facts and weave differing stories from them. Our desires influence how we weigh and interpret the evidence.

Another logical leap can be made when we subconsciously seek or give more weight to evidence that supports our own conclusions. Researchers call this *confirmation bias*. It's always a temptation to favor any data that affirms our previously drawn conclusions and discount the rest.

Scientists guard against drawing false conclusions by carefully documenting their methodology, then submitting the results to others for review by means of a published paper. In other words, they show their work. So one of the ways you can interrogate a story is to ask someone else to examine it.

When you "show your work," explaining to someone else why you believe what you do, you move from subjective to objective. You have to demonstrate how you drew your conclusion.

As an added value, you'll also gain a better understanding of your own story. Explaining your view to others will force you to think through it in ways you wouldn't on your own. Your brain will make logical leaps and accept incongruities that others might not. What's obvious to you probably won't be to them. This exposes the logical flaws, latent assumptions, and biases that may exist.

Here are some questions that can help you assess the logic of your own story, or of someone else's:

- What are the assumptions?
- What is the purpose, the end goal?
- What do I want to be true?

- Am I being objective?
- What would an impartial observer say?
- How did we draw that conclusion?
- Is it provable? How would you verify it?
- Can we draw this conclusion from the facts we have?

Scrapping Bad Stories

When my coach confronted me (Michael) about my explanation for missing the budget, she helped me interrogate my story. Notice how she did it.

First, she acknowledged I had some facts on my side: retail traffic, gas prices, and the rest. But she immediately relativized their importance and how I imagined they fit together.

In my story, they were determinative. In her reconstruction, they were "factors," that is, details that had an impact but weren't by themselves responsible for the outcome. In other words, my x didn't cause y, and she called me on it.

Then, to drive home the point, she reminded me that we were always facing those same or similar factors. "Let's be honest," she said. "It's always tough, right?"

The note about honesty is humorous in retrospect. I was fooling myself and she knew there was some part of me that was in on the con. We mentioned why at the start of chapter 3: I was trying to preserve my image with my board. I didn't want them to doubt my leadership.

That's what my coach homed in on next. I had some facts, but I had misunderstood how they fit together. And I was missing one crucial detail, which she dropped in her bombshell question: "What is it about your leadership that led to this outcome?"

Let's rewrite the formula: $x + my\ leadership = y$. Interrogating my story dismantled my excuse for missing the prior month, but it simultaneously restored my ability to change the outcome next month. I couldn't do anything about the external environment, but I could get creative with my leadership.

By showing me the missing fact, my coach helped me scrap a disempowering story and do something different. The truth will set you free.

THIS WAS THE CASE for Michele as well. I (Megan) was able to work with Michele on overcoming my public speaking paralysis because Michele had successfully interrogated her story following her recovery from cancer. Like Hugh Herr, she wasn't about to accept the story her situation seemed to hand her.

We asked her about her process. "I listed all the things that I thought made a good communicator," said Michele, "vocal quality, good diction, and all the rest. Then I asked, 'Is that accurate? Is that what makes good communication?'" She was establishing the facts.

"I went down the list," she continued. "One after another, I said, 'No,' 'no,' 'no.' I don't really need to have a perfect voice or perfect enunciation to be a great communicator. I was thinking of myself as a great speaker, which is something different. A great communicator needs to be empathetic, truthful, insightful, passionate. And I am *still* all those things. I am a communicator."

Michele's basic approach is one we can all follow when interrogating our story. She stated the facts of her reality. She questioned whether she had all the facts and how they fit together. And based on that, she determined whether her story was accurate.

That became the turning point in her life. Her ideas about what it meant to be a communicator were inadequate. That flawed thinking led to a false belief: "My career as a communicator is over." By rigorously interrogating her story, Michele was able to lay the groundwork for change.

SIX

The Ups and Downs of Intuition

How did the race driver know when to brake? As the Formula One car approached the turn, he mashed the pedal down. Normally, he would have maintained his speed and rocketed through.

Instead, he slowed just in time to avoid joining an unseen pileup of cars around the bend. That instant action probably saved his life; it certainly saved his vehicle. But when asked about the incident later, he couldn't explain why he hit the brakes. He only knew the urge to stop was very strong, even stronger than his desire to win the race.

Later on, a team of psychologists examined him, showing him video of the race so that he could actually relive the moment. Only then did he realize why he'd stopped. The crowd, which would normally have been watching him approach the bend, was looking the other way—frozen in place. They'd witnessed the crash around the turn and were glued to the horror, car after car careening into wreckage.

One detail amiss: the crowd's gaze pointed the wrong direction. That was all the driver's subconscious needed to trigger the desire to brake.

"He didn't consciously process this," said Leeds University Business School professor Gerard Hodgkinson, writing about the incident, "but he knew something was wrong and stopped in time." Intuition protected him from harm, possibly death.[1]

WHEN I (MICHAEL) WAS CEO at Thomas Nelson Publishers, we spent half a million dollars every year to attend an annual trade show. It was a major event. But one day something occurred to me: We participated every year without question. We invested again and again without slowing to ask whether it was the best use of our resources. Everyone assumed it was an essential expenditure. After all, our key partners and vendors would be there, competitors too.

But I wondered: Was it really essential? Any time someone says this or that thing "has to be," it's probably untrue. Very few things are fixed in stone. And when we say they are, it's usually the Narrator floating a faulty story. Even when something is tangible and concrete, we can see it differently from the person standing right next to us.

I doubted our assumptions about the trade show would hold up once we reopened the case. I had the finance team pull the numbers for me. Then I had stakeholders explain what we got from our attendance.

This is the same basic process we looked at in chapter 5. I separated the *whats* from the *whys*. When you break stories down into their components, you test the connections and see whether the story serves the goal as well as people assume.

There were great reasons to move forward, but there were even better reasons to rethink the event based on the goal itself: casting vision and aligning with authors, vendors, and other partners.

When I reviewed the facts for the trade show, I found that we could host our own event, a conference with breakouts and meetings, for 20 percent of what we'd been spending at the trade show. And everyone's attention would be exclusively ours for the event.

Note my process so far: I gathered all the relevant facts I could. I teased out all the assumptions so we could reassess the conclusions in light of our ultimate purpose. I did this collaboratively. We'll talk more about that in chapter 9, but I wanted to get multiple perspectives. And based on that input I had a decision to make.

Yes or no?

Data will not always get you to 100 percent certainty on your decision, even after you've consulted with stakeholders and other interested parties. Maybe the combination of those inputs gets you to 60, 70, 80 percent certainty. Based on the risks and rewards, we often have to trust our gut.

In this chapter we're going to look at intuition, which can be a valuable tool in both interrogating our old stories and creating new ones. In some cases, it's the only tool available. It's also a tool with some serious risks we must factor in.

Let's Define It

As we saw in chapter 2, our brain does a tremendous amount of processing under the line of consciousness. Our unconscious mind is always running, always connecting dots, finding patterns, and helping us answer the what's-next question.

Since our conscious awareness lags behind this unceasing activity of the unconscious mind, we often know things before we can articulate or explain them. We know something is wrong, for instance, when everyone's eyes are looking the wrong direction; it's best to hit the brakes.

We also know when a business risk seems like a good idea, even though you can't prove it'll work in advance. It's as if the Narrator says, "I can't explain. Just trust me."

A gut feeling is not a gift or psychic power. Intuition is knowledge you can't quite explain. It is an inclination to trust or distrust a particular story in the absence of demonstrable proof. It's a kind of knowing generated by your brain, just like reasoning, though it's automatic instead of analytic.

Your brain generates predictions all day long. They come from your subconscious mind and are based on your existing storehouse of concepts and stories. The brain's big project, as we've seen, is to represent whatever you need from the world in your mind so you can think, move, and navigate successfully, moment to moment.[2]

In the case of intuition, it is a prediction based on neural connections that you're not yet fully aware of. You know that you know something. You just don't know why—or usually care.

If we had to factor in every movement and assumption consciously, we couldn't even walk down the sidewalk without being paralyzed by the effort. We don't have enough bandwidth. It's far more efficient to let the unconscious mind handle it while thinking about the stuff we need to: what's for lunch, what time the meeting starts, what to wear to the reception, what the boss meant by that last email, whether to take a vacation day on Friday, and on and on and on.

Both types of knowledge are valid, and both are important. "Humans clearly need both conscious and non-conscious thought processes, but it's likely that neither is intrinsically 'better' than the other," says Hodgkinson.[3]

Interestingly, some highly intuitive thinkers arrived at the same conclusion long before the age of neuroscience. René Decartes, the mathematician and scientist who is also widely regarded as one of the founders of modern philosophy, stated that we rely on two types of understanding to acquire knowledge: intuition and deduction.[4]

Immanuel Kant agreed: "Intuition and concepts constitute . . . the elements of all our knowledge, so that neither concepts without an intuition in some way corresponding to them, nor intuition without concepts, can yield knowledge."[5] Clearly, reason and intuition are both needed for understanding, and your brain makes use of both.

INTUITION ANSWERS THE QUESTION, "What is most likely true?" or "What is most likely to happen next?" To understand how intuition helps us, we can compare it to the standard of proof required in a court of law.

In a criminal case, the prosecution must demonstrate proof beyond reasonable doubt. That's what you're doing when you interrogate a story. You're looking for evidence that would either support or contradict it. While you can't always be 100 percent certain, you can be reasonably sure that some stories are either true or false, helpful or unhelpful.

If you're launching a business, getting married, or investing your life's savings, you want high confidence in the story you're

Reason and intuition are both needed for understanding, and your brain makes use of both.

believing. Do we have a solid business plan that will work in this market? Can I commit myself to a lifelong relationship with this person? Is this financial advisor trustworthy?

In these cases, you want to be able to answer, "Yes, definitely." If you can't, you'll keep interrogating until you've removed any reasonable doubt. For this kind of knowing, we use the analytical function of our minds.

In a civil case, the standard of proof is different. The plaintiff need only prove a preponderance of evidence in their favor. In other words, they need only show that it's more likely that they're right than wrong.

Was this accident caused by negligence? Can we be absolutely sure? Maybe not. But if it seems that it *probably* resulted from negligence, you can find for the plaintiff. In the absence of clear proof, you have to rely on your gut. Your intuition comes into play in cases when you cannot demonstrate the exact reason you know something.

In daily life, you rely on intuition more often than you think. Will the gravel on the highway make you lose traction? Is this salesperson telling me the truth? Do you have enough time to finish this project before lunch? It's hard to say for sure, but your mind will always make a prediction based on what it knows. That's intuition.

To make use of your whole brain, you need to trust your intuition. And to use it wisely, you must understand how it operates so you can easily determine when it's steering you right and when it may be off base.

Knowing beyond Thinking

Intuition can be valuable for interrogating stories, because it gives you a bottom-line assessment of the problem or question.

Take cases of complexity with loads of data, interconnected details, shifting definitions, and the like. In some cases, our brain's executive function will piece together a plausible story to keep us oriented, even if it turns out to be incorrect. In other cases, we can be so overwhelmed by the data we don't know what to think.[6]

Your subconscious mind operates differently, however. Remember that it's constantly searching your story library, looking for possible connections, trying one neural pathway and then another to see if anything clicks. This allows you to form conclusions before your conscious mind can fully state them or the reasons for them (see chap. 3).

These findings are delivered to you as intuition. In the case of a complex story or data-intensive context, your intuition may simply tell you, "No, this is not the time to move forward," or "Yes, we should go all in this quarter."

People use all sorts of phrases to describe when they know something intuitively, everything from "I've got a check in my spirit" to "My gut tells me . . ." Whether we "feel" right or wrong or unsure, science writer Annie Murphy Paul refers to this kind of awareness as "thinking with sensations."[7]

This is less precise than a decision formed through reason, but not necessarily less accurate. Intuition usually serves up a yes-or-no answer, not a highly nuanced and detailed rationale—which would betray more analytic than automatic thinking. This binary feedback comes in handy whenever we face complicated situations with unmanageable or unreliable information.[8]

Consider moments where you're being heavily influenced by others. A skilled salesman, an emotional family member, or an excited neighbor can advance their story very convincingly. By emphasizing some data and ignoring selected other points, they may make their story appear unquestionably true.

As you listen to the spiel, you may have doubts. Don't dismiss them. Our intuition can alert us when something is amiss in someone's pitch or plea. Even if you can't articulate why, your intuition often knows when a story simply doesn't hold up.

In other cases, you may have done all the interrogation you reasonably can but are still left with some uncertainty. After performing a thorough vetting process and identifying three probable candidates for a position, which one should you hire? Dithering over the decision will only delay progress. And another round of interviews may not bring more certainty. You may need to rely on intuition and keep moving.

In other cases, there is simply no time to react to your circumstances. In those cases, intuition is vital.

"People usually experience true intuition when they are under severe time pressure or in a situation of information overload or acute danger, where conscious analysis of the situation may be difficult or impossible," says Hodgkinson. Your gut may be most reliable in these pressure-filled situations.[9]

SOME OF THE STORIES we rely on have a great deal riding on them. Yet no matter how high the stakes, certainty can be as elusive as ever. There may be so much data that it creates more confusion than certainty, or there may be too little information. Either way, you may still need to make a choice.

When I (Megan) prepared to take the CEO role of our company, I remember reading an article in *Harvard Business Review* about what effective executives do differently from ineffective leaders. While being mindful of the problem of principles that don't travel well (see the last chapter), I'm always looking to learn.

In this case, one stat hooked my attention. The researchers interviewed a CEO who said that he feels comfortable making decisions when he has not 90 percent of the information, not 80 percent, not even 70 percent.

"Once I have 65% certainty around the answer, I have to make a call," he said. He checks his thinking against a circle of advisors and then pulls the trigger. "I ask myself two questions," he said. "First, what's the impact if I get it wrong? And second, how much will it hold other things up if I don't move on this?"[10]

This sort of balance is essential. We're going to make mistakes. But we need to fail in the right direction as often as possible. Holding back and refusing to decide in the light of insufficient information feels like safety, but there are costs to not moving forward, just as there are for moving wrongly.

Overall, it's best to make the call, while recognizing that most decisions are not irreversible or unmodifiable. If you screw up, you can usually fix it. And for reasons we'll discuss in chapter 8, even mistakes can be beneficial. Even the wrong step can sometimes help you make the next jump.

When I (Michael) decided on the trade show, I didn't have all the information. I had a gut instinct. I decided to pull out of the industry event and host our own. At a fraction of the cost, we paid for our top customers to join us in our own space with our best authors. The event was a huge success, a hundred times more effective than the original event.

But let me say this: It could have failed. The facts still left plenty up for debate. Given everything we've said so far about interrogating our stories, we need to be aware that intuition can sometimes lead us off the track.

Downsides

Intuition is a form of knowledge. It is sometimes the only knowledge available to us, and it is usually reliable. After all, you're a generally successful human being who has made it this far in life. Chances are good your intuition has served you better than not.

But not always. There are limits to our intuition, and we must keep those limits in mind when interrogating our stories.

For one thing, your intuition is based on your assumptions, your library of existing stories. And as we've mentioned, your stories are based on your experience. Therefore, your intuition is always limited by your experience, which we know can never give us a complete picture of reality. After all, we haven't been everywhere or done everything, nor will we.

This means your intuition will be less reliable in areas where you have little or no experience. The two of us are both experienced in the world of business. We have reasonably good intuition when it comes to finances, marketing, staffing, and so on. But neither of us has any medical background. Our intuition would not be terribly helpful in diagnosing a rare illness.

> Beware trusting your gut too much in contexts where you have little or no experience.

So it makes sense to rely most on our intuition when dealing with concepts and contexts where we have a higher degree of familiarity. Beware trusting your gut too much in contexts where you have little or no experience.

GUT REACTIONS are a manifestation of our go-to stories. They are often well-worn neural pathways, like ruts in the road. We can drift into them without any conscious awareness. Our choice or decision seems obvious and sensible, but it's just an old story tacked onto a new set of circumstances in which it may—or may not—apply.

Our intuition, reflecting as it does our experience and existing stories, is never truly objective. But when our gut reaction is skewed positively or negatively by our preconceived ideas, it is more about prejudice than intuition.

Race and culture are prime examples of this tendency. All of us are conditioned to some degree by an affinity to those who are like us and suspicion of those who are different. Therefore, a person's race, national origin, political views, and other factors may generate a response in us that we take to be intuition. In fact, it could be personal bias based on our familial and cultural formation.

Certain keywords also trigger an automatic response that may be less intuitive than reactive. Advertisers and propagandists have known this for a long time. Your "feeling" that a product may be good or that an economic or political theory may be harmful might be a Pavlovian reaction to terms loaded with meaning, like *value*, *quality*, *elite*, and *proven*, or *tree hugger*, *gas guzzler*, *patriotic*, and *unpatriotic*. Our goals have a similar effect on our thinking. They can cause us to fixate on the things we desire and ignore any evidence that doesn't support our goal.

When relying on intuition, it's critical to distinguish between what we strongly believe or wish to be true and what is most likely to be true. This calls for a rigorous practice of self-awareness to expose our own biases and desires, which are usually hidden from us.

You can also test your intuition by submitting it to the opinion of others, especially those who see things with a different perspective from yours. We'll talk more about the role of others in our thinking in chapter 9.

Using Our Intuition

Intuition and reason are two forms of knowing. Either one can arrive at the right answer. But the best situation is when both are in agreement.

We love stories such as the one about the detective who pursued a hunch despite evidence to the contrary, resulting in the real criminal being brought to justice. Or the story of the visionary CEO who ignored the critics and succeeded in building a towering company. Sometimes your intuition is right and the commonsense interpretation of the facts is wrong. But honestly, that's rare.

I (Megan) found this out the hard way when I had a strong hunch that a particular candidate was the right person for a key position in our company. This person was to play a critical role in launching a new product, so it was important to find a good fit.

We had zeroed in on a candidate, and I was sure this was the right person. We had one last box to check—an instrument we use in hiring called the Kolbe A Index. This tool assesses how well a person's work style aligns with the job at hand. The methodology is highly reliable, having been proven over forty years.

Unfortunately, the score indicated that our prime candidate was a poor fit for the position. My advisor at Kolbe Corp warned me against hiring. But my gut told me this was the right choice. I just *knew* it.

Alas, no. Within a few months, my sure pick realized he was not cut out for the position and accepted a job elsewhere. I'd mistaken my urgency to fill the position for intuition. Good came out of the situation, but—*ouch!*—it was a painful lesson.

This is why an executive making a call with limited information is foolish to do so without first bouncing the decision off advisors. We can supplement that advice by implementing helpful rules of thumb from social psychologist John Bargh, who has studied the unconscious mind for decades.

Don't rely on your gut alone whenever you can interrogate your Narrator. Take a moment of conscious reflection. Pause and poke a bit. Along with that, keep the scale in mind. The bigger the gamble, the greater the need to check your gut. "Don't take big chances for small gains," says Bargh. Finally, don't rely on your gut when it comes to people unless you've got real experience with them.[11]

This does not mean there will never be a time when intuition trumps data. However, those times will be rare. And the data that intuition *never* overrides is the results of your story; the proof is, as they say, in the pudding.

Before you take action on your story, no one knows for sure what the result will be. Afterward, you do know. It was risky to persist in hiring a candidate when I had strong evidence that indicated my story was wrong. However, if I would have persisted in my choice after it was obvious that the candidate just wasn't working, that would have been downright foolish.

INTUITION IS NOT A SIXTH SENSE. It's something better, a function of your brain ceaselessly scanning your environment to find relevant connections. It is a form of knowing that can cut to the bottom line of a situation, enabling you to make a decision when time or data is in short supply.

As you learn to trust your brain, you'll gain greater confidence in yourself and your own thinking. But, of course, stay vigilant so you know when it's time to lean into intuition and when it's simply your Narrator serving you convenient stories that ultimately work against you.

SEVEN

Trading Certainty for Results

Maybe it's a stereotype, but when we think of risk-takers, engineers are low on the list. Engineers work in the realm of specifics, equations, and narrow tolerances. Black-and-white thinking is part of the job—otherwise, things stop working, catch fire, fall down, float away, fizzle out, come apart, overheat, or blow up.

Becoming engineers was the goal when George Kurian and his twin brother, Thomas, left southern India in 1986. Their dad was a chemical engineer working in Kerala. The brothers decided to follow in his footsteps while venturing far from home. Six months into an engineering program in India, the brothers secured partial rides to Princeton University and left for New Jersey.

They had to work part-time jobs to cover their costs, but both graduated with degrees in electrical engineering. From there, they supported each other through business school at Stanford. And after winding paths through several companies—each spent time at Oracle—today both are CEOs, Thomas at Google Cloud and George at the data storage giant NetApp.[1]

George took the top seat at NetApp in 2015, and he inherited a mess. The board asked the prior CEO to resign, and operating margins were less than half of what investors had been promised. A year after taking the helm, George had to lay off almost 1,500 employees to get the business back on track. But under his leadership, NetApp rebounded. Revenues jumped and profits quadrupled. Several years later the company remains strong.

George credits the company's relentless focus and execution for their success. "We have weekly meetings where we review our priorities and keep track of where we are," he said in an interview. Corrective action happens immediately after problems are spotted.

"We want to make decisions at pace," he said, "with sufficient information but not necessarily all information. That speed is absolutely necessary in this industry." And right about now you're probably thinking what we are.

Speed like that can be unsettling. How do you know what's right, if it'll work, if you can afford it, if you can deliver it on time? How does an engineer go from painstakingly double-checking all his formulas to getting comfortable with limited information and making decisions under time constraints?

"With engineering, there's often a black-or-white answer," George said when reflecting on that question. "But as an executive, that's much rarer."

Thanks to the example of his brother and his father, who also found his way into management of a company back in India, George saw it was possible. "They taught me that the breadth of things an executive has to deal with is wider than that of an engineer," he said. "If you wait for certainty, you're almost always too late."[2]

There were a lot of critical, doubtful voices when George Kurian took the helm at NetApp. If he had accepted those stories, he would have failed. There were more voices and stories when he looked at the P&L and decided layoffs were the answer. And still more when the company changed strategic directions. And still more every time something didn't work as planned.

Somewhere in the process, probably beginning without his awareness when he took the gamble to leave home for Princeton and reinforced by his supportive family, George learned a story of his own: You don't have to have all the answers to be effective. You don't have to be certain to be successful.

If you find the idea of examining your stories intimidating, even to the point of questioning and revising some long-held ideas, you're not alone. It's daunting to consider that some of your cherished beliefs about yourself, others, and the world may not be entirely accurate—especially when you don't know what you'll do as a result of changing your story.

Raise the question and it feels like life might stop working, catch fire, fall down, float away, fizzle out, come apart, overheat, or blow up. That's even more true when we begin to evaluate stories about our own lives, choices, careers, and relationships. This creates uncertainty, and your brain is not a fan of uncertainty.

The Narrator is trying to tell you what's next. It doesn't like to admit, "I don't know." Still, it's essential for us to make some version of the shift Kurian made if we're going to challenge the Narrator. We need to learn to tolerate the discomfort of uncertainty to reap the rewards of interrogating our stories.

WE'VE DISCOVERED a few common objections that hinder many of us from critiquing our own thoughts and embracing new ideas. Unable to dispense with the Narrator's go-to stories, we find ourselves locked in place with the inability to find new solutions.

The more important or treasured a story is, the harder it is to question, let alone abandon. When we believe we are right about something, we stick to it. That's not because we lack humility, though that may be a factor. There are neuroscientific and psychological reasons why this process of challenging the Narrator is deeply unsettling.

Some of these reasons have been mentioned already. For example, our stories *feel* true to us. We may actually feel queasy at the thought of abandoning them. Other reasons involve how our brains operate.

Your brain is like a shark, constantly patrolling its territory day after day. But rather than looking for food, your brain is looking for meaning. It's trying to understand your environment so it can answer the question, "What happens next?" The more certain your brain is that it understands what's happening, the better it feels. So it avoids potentially disruptive activities such as rethinking your life.

Yet risk itself is not a bad thing. It's unavoidable. Life is unpredictable. There's a certain level of uncertainty attached to everything we do. When we take on a calculated risk, there's always the prospect of something better on the other side. You leave one job to seek a better one. You invest money in a business to produce a profit. You engage in a relationship to experience love.

Each of those activities involves uncertainty, but each carries the potential for even greater benefits. Something good stands on the other side of risk. That's what makes it worth taking.

When it comes to examining your current thinking to find new and creative solutions, you're bound to encounter uncertainty. That'll be uncomfortable, and we might as well discuss why. When we recognize our triggers, it's a lot easier to ignore them and press on with the work of interrogating the Narrator.

Survival of the Surest

The purpose of this book is to help you think better so you can achieve better results in your life. To do that we're leveraging the basic mechanics of the human brain, which have to do with survival.

While it sounds simple to say that if you change your thoughts it will improve your outcome, your subconscious doesn't see it that way. To your brain, stories are all about keeping you alive and well.

Ice = Slippery. Step around it.
Stranger = Danger. Don't get in that car.
Sugar and fat = Good. Eat all you can.

While that last one doesn't work so well in an age of abundance, your association of certain foods with pleasure is one of the original human stories. In a context where food was hard to come by, humans needed an incentive to eat the things that would keep them alive. Storing fat was essential because we couldn't be certain where our next meal was coming from. So our brains coded the connection between foods containing sugar and fat with pleasure.[3]

For many of us today, the overabundance of foods containing sugar and fat has become a problem. We're storing too much of it. But we can't seem to turn off the connection between fat- and sugar-rich foods and a tasty meal. The story isn't working for many of us, but we're stuck with it. That story is hardwired into the brain, preloaded into every new human as part of our survival instinct.

While we're urging you to challenge your stories, including some that you've held for a long time, your subconscious is shouting, "No, no, no! Danger! Danger!"

That makes it difficult to abandon our stories about anything of importance, such as relationships, family, politics, money, or success, even when we may realize our stories are no longer helping us thrive. We have a built-in aversion to changing our minds. That's just your brain trying to keep you safe.

That's part of what was going on for me (Megan) as I re- sisted public speaking. I saw my friend fall apart. I felt my own adrenaline surge when I imagined the spotlight, real or figurative. Speaking could kill me. That's what the Narrator said. Besides, speaking would reveal to everyone what I feared: that something was deeply wrong with me. I needed to avoid that at all costs.

Beyond that basic instinct for self-protection, challenging our stories is difficult because it threatens to unravel our sense of meaning. By questioning the basic ways we understand the world, we question everything we know.

Stories are meaning-making devices, and they're all con- nected. Tugging at the thread of one story may call another into question, and another and another. Where will it end? Is there *nothing* we can count on? That's a frightening thought.

When we face these moments of new awareness that chal- lenge our view of reality, we experience what psychologists call *existential anxiety*. That's the uncomfortable feeling that your entire life has been called into question.

WAY BACK IN 1849, Danish philosopher Søren Kierkegaard predicted this would happen on a broad scale when the prevailing worldview—the collective story of Western civilization—proved inadequate to make sense of the new challenges in a world that was changing faster than ever before.[4]

He was right. As a field, psychiatry grew rapidly through the next century, paralleling the huge social changes brought on by industrialization and helping people cope. Today, 42 percent of adults are or have been in some form of counseling or therapy.[5]

The most common presenting problem is depression, which is often connected to a major life event such as grief or illness that results in a deep questioning of life's meaning. So if the idea of rethinking your stories about life, business, relationships, and even reality makes you a bit anxious, you've got lots of company. That's how the human psyche responds to an existential crisis.

The good news here is that these reactions reveal something important about you. They show that you are engaging with these concepts at a deep level. The fact that you're raising mental objections demonstrates that you're at least willing to explore new ideas.

And the anxiety you feel is proof that you understand the implications of interrogating your story. It could certainly mean changing things in your life. You're thinking deeply, and that's vital for learning and growth.

To overcome anxiety on this point, verbalize your fear. (After all, it's just another story your Narrator is telling you.) Ask yourself, "What's the worst that can happen?" Honestly, the worst possibility is that you don't find the exercise helpful and remain right where you are.

On the other hand, the best that can happen is that you gain a clearer understanding of your situation and new, more effective ways to deal with it. Reexamining your understanding of reality is an opportunity for positive change. You may well determine that your story is correct and worth keeping. But the exercise itself will strengthen your ability to solve problems and achieve your goals.

Are You Saying Nothing Is Really True?

Another objection we commonly hear is that challenging our stories is somehow denying reality or suggesting that nothing is finally, utterly true. It seems to say we all have to create our own version of reality. If yours doesn't work for you, make up something else.

That's not what we're saying. We may disagree on what to call a rock. We may use that rock for different things and see it as different colors. But when we stub our toe on it, we'll both trip. Clearly, we are all encountering something real.

What we are saying is that our ability to know what we're dealing with and make sound judgments is not as solid as we think.

Remember, our stories are formed of what we've earned by direct (but limited) experience or learned indirectly from the (similarly limited) experience of others. Some of that is tested and true. A lot of it's not. But, either way, how we understand and act on those stories is open to interpretation and the needs of the moment or situation. As we saw in chapter 5, even proven principles don't always apply beyond their original context.

We should exercise a bit of humility about what we think we know and be willing to rethink the connections between things when presented with new evidence. That's always hard

Reexamining your understanding of reality is an opportunity for positive change.

for humans to do, and it's made harder still by the way we've been trained to think over the past several hundred years.

Since the Enlightenment, the twin philosophies of empiricism and rationalism have provided the intellectual foundation for most of our institutions. Together, they argue that (a) we can know the world through the senses, and (b) we can validate that knowledge through rational thought.

Later, the Industrial Revolution brought an intense focus on and optimism about the ways science and technology can improve our understanding of the world. We arrived at the popular belief, now almost universally held, that by using scientific inquiry and logic, we can know—or will eventually know—everything about what the world is and how it works.

That's an oversimplification, of course. But the point is that we have had a growing confidence in our ability to be absolutely certain of what is true. Is that confidence well placed?

CONSIDER WHAT WAS ARGUABLY the pivotal case for advancing the value of science over other forms of "knowing" in the Western world: the debate about what lies at the center of the universe.

Nikolaus Copernicus was a Renaissance-era mathematician, astronomer, and Catholic priest. In the days when nearly everyone believed that the sun revolved around the earth—because that's what we seem to see happening every day—Copernicus proposed that the sun, rather than Earth, is the center of the universe.

The publication of this idea in *On the Revolutions of the Celestial Spheres* in 1543 triggered the Copernican Revolution, eventually dethroning the previously held view of the world.

Today, only a few fringe thinkers argue that the earth is the center of the universe. Yay, science! But wait.

Today no one agrees with Copernicus that the sun is at the center of the universe. That story was overturned in 1610. Using a telescope, Galileo discovered that the earth and sun are both part of the Milky Way galaxy, which contains all the stars in the universe. Of course, we've since rewritten that story too.

In 1924, Edwin Hubble, using a much more powerful telescope, proved that many stars were far too distant to be part of the Milky Way and that there are entire galaxies outside our own. Many galaxies, it turns out. As recently as a decade ago, astronomers estimated the universe contained 200 billion galaxies, give or take. More recent research indicates there are probably ten times that number.[6]

Copernicus, Galileo, and Hubble were all hailed for their discoveries, which, in their day, seemed to be perfect explanations for what we see in the sky. Yet their stories illustrate the most overlooked truth about knowledge, regardless of how it's acquired: knowledge is always limited and provisional.

We simply don't know everything. Despite our best intentions, our stories about the world are often wrong, or at least incomplete.

This doesn't mean that scientific inquiry is not to be trusted or that logical conclusions may be safely ignored. It simply means that our ability to know exactly what's happening in the world is always imperfect. While it may be partly correct and somewhat helpful, it is seldom on-the-dot right.

If that was the case for Copernicus and Galileo, how much more is it the case for us when reading a financial statement, observing a customer focus group, or listening to a family member or friend? We never have all the data.

NEARLY EVERYONE has an innate sense that some things are absolutely true. And we agree. Some stories should not be rewritten. For example, our sense of right and wrong, like our survival instinct, comes preloaded.

Admittedly, that story varies a bit from culture to culture and has been completely overwritten in some individuals' minds. Even the best of us occasionally try to rewrite our sense of justice based on personal desires or biases.

Yet our stories about murder, stealing, and lying, for example, have been mostly reliable and stable over time and across cultures.[7] Nothing we're suggesting is a license to rewrite the basic moral and ethical framework that exists in nearly all societies. Some stories are absolutely true, meaning they apply everywhere, all the time.

But there are fewer of those than you might think. Most cultures recognize this, as do the world's major religions. Judaism and Christianity have just ten commandments. The Apostles' Creed has twelve articles. Buddhism rests on eight precepts, Islam on five pillars. Even with those small numbers of absolutes, adherents may still disagree on what they actually mean.

Here again it's wise to maintain a degree of humility about what we know for sure. When we mistake the many things about which we can't be absolutely certain for the few about which we can, we get stuck. Our minds are locked against the new ideas that could well provide valuable solutions to our problems.

To overcome anxiety on this point, narrow your list of unquestionable thoughts or beliefs to true essentials. When facing any situation, ask yourself, "Can I say without bias that this problem presents a clear moral or ethical imperative?" If not, you should be able to interrogate your view of the problem. In other words, you're free to imagine a better story.

Tugging the Sweater String

Many of our stories are deeply interconnected. Just like our brains establish stories by linking one concept to another, we elaborate on those connections, forming conclusions that become components in additional stories.

Many stories are contingent on each other like blocks in a wall, or strands in a web. This is most true of our fundamental stories, which tend to be complex. At some level, we realize that if we pull one block from the base, the entire structure will lack integrity.

That latent fear keeps us from examining some ideas too closely. They seem true because they have to be true. If not, then our entire frame of thought will be altered.

This includes our ideas of political theory, religious belief, family systems, educational philosophy, management, and economics. But it can also involve how we think about work, handle our to-do lists, or rest on the weekends.

The two of us sometimes see this in meetings of our executive team. If we're meeting to address a problem, we may start pulling the sweater string. And once we start we're not always sure where we'll end up, because our assumptions, goals, and preferred strategies represent a large network of interconnected concepts and connections.

When we begin to unravel one story, we may see, rightly or wrongly, implications for others. In our experience, this is sometimes frustrating but almost always fruitful. Experiencing friction when pursuing a goal sometimes points to larger, deeper challenges we've missed or papered over with other stories. It's better to accept the uncertainty that comes with realizing you have a problem than pretend you don't.

> It's better to accept the uncertainty that comes with realizing you have a problem than pretend you don't.

How do we respond when things seem like they're all unraveling before our eyes (whether they are or we only imagine it)? We often shut down. We may immediately close off any conversation or line of thinking that seems threatening.

That's a big mistake. It effectively stops us in our tracks, ensuring we never think differently about our problem or find a better solution.

"THERE IS A THOUGHT that stops thought," said G. K. Chesterton. "That is the only thought that ought to be stopped."[8] When we continue to interrogate, we keep ourselves open to solutions. And if that opens up new problems, so be it. Progress is wobbly.

Amazon founder Jeff Bezos is well known for changing his mind, for interrogating and—looking ahead to part 3 now—reimagining his stories based on new information. He seems able to disentangle one story from the others so that changing his mind on a particular issue or project doesn't threaten his entire way of thinking.

Consider the failed venture Amazon Auctions. It was launched to compete with eBay, but the Amazon approach never gained traction. Rather than seeing the loss of this one story—*we can go head-to-head with eBay in the auction space*—as a threat to the entire business, Bezos changed the story and his strategy.

The result was Amazon's third-party sellers program, which is massively profitable.[9] It is possible to abandon ideas that seem central to our most important stories without blowing up our entire worldview. The slippery slope is not quite as slick as we sometimes imagine.

It's true that rewriting stories will call others into question, but this is another story the Narrator tells us to keep us from perceived-but-imaginary harm—more fear than reality.

Most of our stories are more like a web than a wall. In a wall each brick depends on the others for its stability. Take out one brick, and it weakens the entire structure. Remove one near the foundation, and the entire thing may collapse.

Webs are different. The strands are interconnected, but there are various points of contact between them. If one strand is removed, the web as a whole will be largely unaffected. Most of our stories are like that. They have certain concepts in common, but rewriting one does not mean that all related stories have to be abandoned. Sometimes by replacing one story with another, we actually strengthen the web.

To overcome anxiety on this point, continue thinking! Resist the temptation to shut down your inquiry. Remain open to new ideas. Keep thinking about the problem at hand.

Uncertainty Signals Possibility

Our goal is to clarify the Narrator's influence on your responses to challenges while pursuing your goals. If you understand this, you can get unstuck and uplevel to something better. If you don't, you'll likely stay right where you are or drift somewhere you don't want to be.

That choice stared me (Megan) in the face as I accepted the challenge to speak. As he mentioned, my dad is a speaker. He's been speaking publicly since I was in diapers. I'm sure people assumed I would be naturally good at it, like it's some kind of genetic transmission.

Deep down, however, I knew I was not a speaker. I'd convinced myself of that. The longer I hid my fear and the more requests I turned down while the scope and demands of my job increased, the greater the shame and fear became. Odds are good you have a similar area in your life.

But the situation became untenable. I didn't like my Narrator's stories, but they felt true. They seemed so true that to question them felt risky. Worse, acting as if they weren't true felt downright dangerous.

But what if my Narrator was misinformed? We rarely have the whole truth. We've all been wrong more often than we could count. But, as we've seen, admitting the possibility of having it wrong, even a bit, is deeply unsettling.

Of course, the possibility we're wrong points to the possibility of something better. It's best to think of uncertainty as a yellow light, not a red one. It means caution. That's wise. But sometimes the only safe course is to plow through the intersection regardless.

That's what I did when I sent the text to Michele. And that's what I did again when my team said they wanted a keynote. I had more work to do. We all do. Once we interrogate our stories and find they don't hold up, we need to imagine a different story. We'll talk about how to do that next in part 3.

For now, let's close out this section on interrogating the Narrator, especially as it relates to the inevitable uncertainty that comes with questioning our stories. After all, success in life often comes down to our tolerance for the discomfort of uncertainty. The greater our capacity for uncertainty, the more creative we can be about the challenges we face.

First, recognize that internal resistance is normal. Rather than tensing up and shutting down, take a look inside. Practice self-awareness by asking, "What am I feeling and why?" Name your emotions, then set them aside temporarily so you can think.

Second, embrace the opportunity for growth. When any meaningful story is called into question, it seems like a threat. To let go of a long-held belief would seem to be a great loss, and we recoil from the prospect. But what if this process is really an opportunity for growth? It usually is.

Uncertainty points to new possibilities. The goal here is to understand your world better so you can make better choices. Remove the anxiety by focusing on the win. You will gain much more than you lose by finding a clearer understanding of your situation.

Third, separate yourself from your story. We often stake a good share of our identity on the stories we create, especially those related to career, success, and professional status. It's helpful to recognize that you have created your stories and not vice versa.

You don't stop being yourself when you reframe your story about wealth, for example, or success, or happiness. If anything, your new story will become even more an expression of your identity. Why? Because it will be closer to the truth than the old one.

Finally, hold your stories with an open hand, not a clenched fist. When you find yourself unwilling to question a concept or connection that forms your story, find out why. Resist the urge to defend at all costs. Ask questions. Your ego is not on trial here. You are seeking a better understanding of your world. That's hard to do while defending your turf.

ACTION

Return to the story you told earlier about your problem or opportunity. Now use the Full Focus Self-Coacher (fullfocus.co /self-coacher) to interrogate it and capture your insights. What are the facts? Are you assuming connections and causes that aren't there? Are you missing any details? If it makes you feel uncertain, congratulations: You might be on the right path.

WHAT MORE WE KNOW

▶ Whatever the story in our head, it's important to ask, *Can we really know this based on the evidence we have? What are the facts versus the conjectures that glue those facts into the story I'm telling myself?*

▶ When we are focused on a particular outcome, we may miss key information that would change the story.

▶ Intuition can be a valuable tool in both interrogating our old stories and creating new ones. But it has some serious risk factors.

▶ Beware trusting your gut too much in contexts where you have little or no experience.

▶ Reexamining your understanding of reality is an opportunity for positive change.

PART 3

IMAGINE

TRAIN YOUR NARRATOR

EIGHT

Different Neurons Tell Different Stories

I (Michael) once attended a conference with attendees from about a dozen countries, representing a wide range of cultures, ethnicities, and religious groups. During the opening session, we were asked to gather in groups of three and create a list of all the things we had in common.

Well, I thought, *that'll be practically nothing.* After all, what could I hope to have in common with people who spoke different languages, held different cultural values, and had vastly different worldviews? Everything I knew, or thought I knew, made me doubt that we'd even be able to communicate. I was prepared for ten minutes of nodding my head, smiling politely, and mentally working on my to-do list.

I was so off base! By the time the exercise concluded, our group of three, each from a different country and religious group, had identified eighty-two things we shared in common.

We all loved our children and wanted a better life for them. We each valued honesty and integrity. We loved to laugh, enjoyed reading, and had some of the same goals. Honestly, I left the session feeling surprised, inspired, and grateful. The experience instantly changed my way of thinking about people from other cultures, and I've never forgotten the lesson.

That day marked a turning point in my journey toward keeping an open mind, one that is ready to consider new ideas and experiences, and willing to form new connections between them. In other words, I became willing to rewrite my stories to more accurately reflect reality.

WHAT WE USUALLY refer to as a closed mind is nothing more than the brain's standard method of operation, which prefers familiar, well-established neural pathways. Our brains excel at identifying patterns and filing them for future use. So when we encounter any situation or experience, the Narrator races into the archive and grabs the most familiar possible story to deal with it.

Our most frequently used neural pathways become like the interstate highways in our brains. They're the fastest, most direct route between any two points—concepts in this case.[1] Why wouldn't we use them? All we have to go on is our existing library of concepts and stories. That's why, when we have reached a settled conclusion on any subject, we have a hard time even seeing another possibility.

This explains my doubtfulness about making connections with people from other cultures at the conference. In the past, I'd had difficulty communicating with people who were very different from me. Since that was my only frame of reference, it never occurred to me that we might have a great deal in common.

To form a different opinion, something had to push me off the familiar route of my existing thoughts. A new experience created a new neural connection in my brain, which made it possible to create a new story: *There is more that connects me than separates me from people of different backgrounds.*

Likewise, if you want to imagine a new story, you must find a way to break free from your existing thought patterns. Remember the basics of how your brain operates. It contains a massive network of nerve cells (neurons) connecting and communicating across synapses. Those neural connections are both the means by which you think and the shaper of what you think.

So if you want to think different thoughts, find a way to get your brain off its familiar pathways to form new neural connections. Once you get off the interstate and take a few back roads, you discover things you'd never see or experience on the main road. Your brain works in much the same way. Force it to think along a different pathway, and it will present you with new thoughts and ideas, which you can use to write a better story with a better outcome.[2]

In this chapter, we'll give you techniques to overcome your brain's reluctance to disrupt its familiar routines. When we're done, you'll have a handful of solid, workable strategies to open your mind and tinker with the neural connections that form your thoughts.

Start with Possibility

In our coaching practice, we often notice that clients have unintentionally closed their minds to new possibilities. It's not surprising. The Narrator places a high value on protecting you from failure and naturally uses the experiences you already have to do so. Perhaps you recognize your own Narrator in self-limiting statements such as these:

- I could never do that.
- We don't have enough resources to start this project.
- The right candidate just doesn't exist.
- I'm not good with technology.
- We'll never win because they cheat.
- You know how *they* are.
- We just don't have time to tackle that problem.
- They'll never hire me.
- I don't have enough money.

Statements like these provide a measure of security because they insulate us from risk and offer a sense of certainty. Even if we are not happy with our circumstances, we can take comfort in knowing that "We don't really have a choice" or "There's nothing we can do." This thinking may quickly answer "what's next?" but it also sets a hard limit on what we believe to be possible. It short-circuits any attempt to remap the connections in our stories, locking us into our existing problems.

Unfortunately, these self-limiting ideas take on even greater power when challenged. When people challenge our assumptions, we defend them. We tend to look for support among those who agree with us and vilify those who disagree. Then we harden our own thinking by associating only with people who agree with us.[3]

Fortunately, your brain is highly flexible. Even though your mindset may seem fixed, it isn't. You can change the default settings in your brain. As educator Jo Boaler put it, "As we begin to realize our potential, we unlock parts of ourselves that had been held back and start to live without limiting beliefs; we become able to meet the small and large challenges we are faced with in life and turn them into achievements."[4] You can train yourself to think in terms of possibility.

So the first advice we give in coaching is to practice self-awareness. Like we talked about in chapter 5, one starting point for interrogating your story is to notice your words and your emotions. Take note of how you respond verbally to situations, problems, or suggestions. If your responses include language that is dismissive, negative, or defensive, ask yourself why. Don't be self-critical. Simply follow your thoughts and see where they lead.

Follow your emotions in the same way, especially negative ones. When you feel anger, fear, anxiety, dread, or hostility, ask why. At the end of that thought train, you'll likely discover a story about yourself, the world, or other people that was created to insulate you from risk rather than advance your goals.

ONCE YOU'VE IDENTIFIED a story that is limiting, the easiest way to replace it is to swap it out for one that is more empowering. Here's an example. If you have a limited mindset and assume demand always outruns supply, you might find yourself saying things like "We don't have enough time" or "We'll never be able to raise the capital for that."

But if you exchange that for a possibility mindset, with a story based on renewable resources, you might instead make statements like "We can achieve more this year than we did last" or "Let's get started, and the resources will follow."

You don't have to be a psychoanalyst to make these exchanges. It's enough to recognize the limits inherent in your thoughts and exchange them for a possibility-based outlook.

Here are some statements that typify a limited mindset, paired with statements that indicate openness to possibility and change. If you can see yourself in any of the limited-mindset statements, begin to replace that thinking with the more positive belief.

Limited Mindset	Possibility Mindset
There's no way around this problem.	Every problem has a workaround.
I don't have the resources.	I'll find the resources I require when I need them most.
There are too many obstacles.	There are more opportunities than obstacles.
I don't know how to go about that.	Somebody has already figured out how to do what I want to do. I just need to locate them.
That's not the way we do things here.	Strategies are meant to be serviceable, not sacred.
I failed. I'm a failure.	Failure is feedback, not a verdict.
I tried that. I'm no good at it.	You don't have to win all the time to succeed in the end.
I don't have enough time.	Constraints liberate more than they limit.

By the way, you don't have to believe the swap at first. Sometimes we can assert a claim and then act as if it's true; then we end up making it real in our actions. It's like reality catches up to our beliefs.[5]

ONE OF OUR FAVORITE coaching techniques—both with clients and with our teammates—is to encourage possibility thinking with open questions. Typically, when people ask questions, they focus on the problem itself. You'll hear questions like: What seems to be the problem? Why did this happen? How could I have prevented this? How much will this cost me?

While those are all valid, they can narrow our focus to the problem and thus the most obvious solutions. In that sense, our questions can limit our imagination. We can think of these as closed questions.

We guide clients and teams with possibility questions. Possibility questions emanate from an imaginative, solutions-oriented mindset. They are a way of developing what psychologist Martin Seligman labeled "learned optimism."[6]

This begins with the idea that our current conclusions about a situation are not the only possible formulation. They're just the best you have at this moment. But there is almost always an alternative way to see it.

A possibility question is any query that takes you beyond an analysis of the problem to a search for new solutions. While there is no finite list of possibility questions, here are some good examples.

- What does this make possible?
- What if I've got it backward?
- What would it take to accomplish x, y, or z?
- How can we reframe this?
- What else could I think?
- How do I want to show up in this situation?
- What is likely to happen in twelve months? Three years? How could we change that?

- Who knows more about this than I do?
- What would have to be true for that to happen?

Notice also that these questions cast the asker in the posture of a learner. Closed questions presume that there is a single right answer to be immediately identified. Possibility questions allow for exploration and discovery, which lie at the heart of imagination. Questions like these light up new neural pathways in the brain.

Push Back

Another technique for forming new thoughts is to push back. It's not by accident that the stereotype of a creative genius is the eccentric contrarian, the person who stands apart from convention, never caring what people think of them or their ideas. Think of Steve Jobs's dogmatic insistence on simplicity or Marie Curie's willingness to defy convention. While that's certainly an exaggerated image of the creative problem solver, it's not entirely wrong.

As it turns out, there's a direct correlation between our ability to think creatively and our willingness to stand apart from normative ways of thinking. As neuropsychologist Elkhonon Goldberg puts it, "Propensity toward nonconformity is certainly not a sufficient prerequisite of creativity, but it is arguably a necessary one."[7]

Psychologist Gary Klein calls this the first route to discovery, that is, to contradict the received story. In other words, to interrogate and deconstruct what others think.[8]

To think creatively, we must be willing to ask the questions no one else is willing to ask, propose the ideas others are too timid to voice, or take the actions that frighten others into passivity. This doesn't mean that creative thinkers must be brash or arrogant or eccentric, only that they be brave enough to think new thoughts.

To think creatively, you must be willing
to ask the questions
no one else is willing to
ask, propose the ideas
others are too timid
to voice, or take the
actions that frighten
others into passivity.

That means pushing back on standard explanations, commonly accepted stories, or "commonsense" interpretations of facts.

PUSHING BACK on commonly accepted stories can sometimes take the form of embracing what might seem to be extreme positions. Many of the most creative minds have done exactly that. *We can send a person to the moon and back in this decade* (John F. Kennedy). *Why can't private companies fly into space* (Richard Branson)*? Let's build the world's biggest theme park in a relatively unknown city in Florida* (Walt Disney).

When we push beyond the boundaries of what is thought to be possible, our minds begin to make new connections, write better stories, and achieve unexpected results. Sometimes the way to spark a breakthrough is to dial your thinking all the way up to "crazy," then pull it back a notch.

Counterfactual thinking is a related technique for pushing back on accepted thinking. Asking questions like "What if we knew we could not fail?" or "What if we had unlimited resources?" or "What if we were starting this business today rather than forty years ago?" can leapfrog your thinking over existing connections and into new possibilities.

Another technique for pushing back against your brain's default way of assessing a situation is to purposely hold contradictory ideas in your mind and let your brain puzzle on how to resolve the difficulty. One study of Nobel laureates, for instance, found they intentionally and actively contemplate paradoxes to help them produce breakthroughs.[9]

This method works because it helps break old storylines and formulate new ones. Contemplating paradoxes forces new neural pathways because the existing pathways don't work to resolve the tension.[10]

We teach our coaching clients to reimagine stories that hold an apparent contradiction by suspending the idea that the solution must be either/or, to look for a third way. Sometimes the best way to make sense of our experience is not to eliminate the idea or detail that doesn't seem to fit but to recast the story in a way that harmonizes or even transcends the contradiction.[11]

Time and time again, the great problem solvers of history have used this method to improve our understanding. That's what Copernicus did, and Galileo, and Hubble. They concluded that the data wasn't wrong. It was the story that explained the data that needed to be changed.

Joy Paul Guilford, a pioneer in the study of creativity, called this technique *divergent thinking*, which is a way of thinking about problems that have no obvious, single answer.[12]

One example of divergent thinking at work is when people deal with a lack of resources on the job. It would be easy to say, "I need x resources to produce y results. I don't have x resources; therefore, I cannot deliver y results." This looks and feels like critical thinking, but it's actually your Narrator just jumping to a conclusion. It's the old neural pathway—a script—providing a predictable and "true-ish" belief about the situation.

But divergent thinking says, "I don't have x resources; however, I can still produce y results." The key is what's happening in the person's mind as they state the paradox. Their brain is now busy trying to imagine how it's possible to do what seems impossible.[13]

Don't give up too easily on concepts that seem to be in conflict. With a bit of divergent thinking and the aid of your subconscious, you might find a connection that will help reimagine your story.

Look for Novelty

But what if you feel stuck? How do you jump-start your creativity to generate new ideas and stories? Let's begin by taking a look at some of the most creative people out there: children.

New ideas are the essence of imagination, and children excel at coming up with new ideas. For example, when the container ship *Ever Given* became wedged in the Suez Canal in 2021, an enterprising reporter asked children for their solutions. The results were novel, to say the least.

Teddy, age four, was certain his idea would work: "They need a crane and a rope and a ramp and a car. The car will run on the ramp and cut the rope and land on the boat with a crash. This will bump the boat back into the sea. If that doesn't work, we could just add another car." Hugo, age five, offered his answer with equal authority: "Cut it!" he said, meaning cut off the corner of the boat.[14]

Novel solutions, to say the least. However, they lacked relevance to the situation. In other words, they would not have worked in solving the problem.

Adults tend to excel at generating relevant ideas, but they usually lack novelty. Remember, the Narrator has access only to your past experience, so ideas tend to be the same ones you've heard before.

This dynamic plagues most brainstorming sessions. Creative director Stefan Mumaw describes the normal process. When a brainstorming session kicks off, everyone tosses out ideas—but they're not terribly novel. And we know why.

Brainstorming is fundamentally a neurological process in which the brain first exhausts familiar pathways before trying to create new connections between existing concepts. At first, your brain rebels against anything that's totally new—to some degree, totally novel ideas aren't even available to your conscious mind at the start. Thankfully, that's just the first stage of thinking through a problem.

As the number of obvious ideas dips, people start getting desperate. Then someone—maybe you—suggests a truly nutty idea. And that's the seed for the breakthrough.

Somehow, stating an idea that is clearly impractical but highly novel frees people to suggest ideas they may have considered too offbeat to mention. It starts pushing the boundaries of what's possible. After that, real creative thoughts begin to emerge. Wrong may not be right, but it could stand just a leap or two away from right, and it might represent the fastest path to the answer you need.

Releasing one crazy idea begins to spark new connections. That's the moment when your brain begins to mix and match concepts, trying to fit them together like pieces of a jigsaw puzzle. And once that process starts, it takes on a life of its own.[15] Here's how Mumaw diagrams the process.

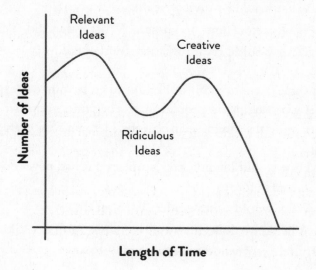

Effective brainstorming depends on recognizing the stages of thought and navigating between them. Don't mistake that first dip for the end of the process. It's merely the prologue for the real creative work.

The key to identifying novel but relevant ideas is to, as Mumaw puts it, "get to stupid faster."[16] Stating the ridiculous idea is effective, because it removes the social inhibition against posing seemingly impractical ideas.

TO SPARK YOUR CREATIVITY, ask questions like these:

- What's the dumbest (or craziest) idea that might actually work?
- What would I do if I were someone else in this situation?
- What would have to be true for us to succeed?
- What would we do if anything were possible?
- What factors limit my choices? What if they didn't exist?
- What would I try if I weren't afraid of failing?

Another way of forcing our brains to go beyond our experience is approaching the problem with a beginner's mindset, asking questions that might seem obvious. Here are a few examples:

- How would I handle this problem if it had never occurred before?
- What would a fifth grader say about this?
- Why do we do it this way?
- Do we still believe that idea?

- What makes others think or behave that way?
- Do I really need to do this? Does anyone?
- If I were starting this business today, would I organize it the way it is now?
- What does that word or phrase really mean?
- How else could you explain this idea?

The simple act of rethinking or restating what you already know will force a reexamination of concepts, connections, and processes that have become like the wallpaper in your living room: invisible.

Neuroscientists, artists, business school professors, psychologists, even classicists point to a basic pattern in creativity or innovation: breaking apart old ideas and either recombining them in new ways or adding outside elements to create new possibilities.[17] But how do you know your new story holds the answer you're after?

Tinker and Experiment

Sometimes the resistance to new thinking comes from others, and sometimes it's internal. We instinctively know the risk of thinking too far outside the box. Nearly three-quarters of change initiatives fail.[18] We're convinced a huge factor is risk aversion. That sets up resistance that virtually dooms the proposed change.

A simple way to overcome that resistance is to adopt an experimental mindset, which sees new ideas as experimental rather than final. This is the essence of the scientific method. A scientist observes a problem, develops a hypothesis, then conducts an experiment to validate the idea. This requires the researcher to hold the idea lightly and avoid drawing firm conclusions until the experimentation is complete.

To develop an experimental mindset, you must shift from thinking, *My ideas about the situation are complete and perfect*, to *This is my best understanding so far. Let's give it a go and see what happens.* This is how all advances are made. From Copernicus to Marie Curie to Jeff Bezos, there are countless examples of people who used new, innovative ideas to reimagine their world.

We can all think of people like this, whether we know them personally or have heard their story in the news. Any successful person you see didn't get where they are by doing the same old thing. They innovated. They adapted. They changed. And you can do the same.

When you think of your new story ideas as experiments, it's easier to try them on and convince others to do the same. Since you can always change your story based on new information, you're not asking yourself or anyone else to commit to it indefinitely.

By labeling a new point of view as an experiment, you communicate that the positive outcome of your idea, not the story itself, is what really matters. If it works, great. If it doesn't work, nobody will be stuck with it. Either way, you'll be able to gather data you would otherwise never have access to. And often enough, mistakes put us closer to the breakthrough, even though they look like failures in the moment.[19]

That's why Uber, for example, ran a major experiment before launching its Express Pool service in 2018. Rather than wondering how the idea would impact its other services, they tried it out.[20] Treating your new story as an experiment reduces the risk and enables others to convince themselves—or not. Either way, you'll know far more at the end of the experiment than you knew at the beginning.

Not surprisingly, many of our first attempts at anything will not produce the desired outcome. As adults, we call that failure, which is a mistake. We should think of it as feedback. That takes the sting out of a less-than-ideal attempt at rewriting your story. And it eliminates the feeling of being stuck. Gaining feedback from the real world is essential for any growth or change.

This means that an element of surprise is essential to the process of rewriting your story. Babies, who probably learn more in a day than adults do in a year, register surprise all the time. Neuroscientist Stanislas Dehaene points out that these unexpected results merely pique their interest and cause them to investigate.

This was demonstrated by researchers who presented children with events that would seem impossible, like a toy passing through a wall. The children would remember the sound it made and play with it for much longer than a comparable toy that hadn't surprised them. They might even make up a word to describe what happened, like, "I bleeked the toy."[21]

This is how we learn. Something happens that we don't understand. We investigate it. We get feedback. We change our conclusions about the situation based on what we've learned. Or, as Dehaene puts it, "Every unexpected event leads to a corresponding adjustment of the internal model of the world."[22] We improve our story.

That's why it's important to reframe our attempts at reimagining a story as feedback rather than failure. Most of us don't like finding out that our ideas don't work. It's discouraging and sometimes embarrassing. Yet it is a vital part of the process of discovery.

The key to reimagining your story is to keep at it. Keep experimenting and iterating, using the feedback you get to refine your thinking. No story is ever complete in that our stories are subject to revision based on new information. The more you learn, the more refined your understanding will become.

ONE CAUTION is in order here. Beware of using your experimentation to affirm your ideas rather than to learn about them. This is a common problem in research. We begin with a hypothesis—or story—which we set out to validate. Generally, we've already invested a good deal of time and energy in the hypothesis.

Naturally, we hope it will be proven true. That can lead us to ignore feedback that doesn't support our story. Or we may try to force the feedback to fit our point of view. As the popular saying goes, if you torture the data long enough, it will confess to anything.[23]

The experimental mindset comes from a desire to discover, not to prove. Perhaps that's what led Nobel laureate Ivar Giaever to say, "To me the greatest moment in an experiment is always just before I learn whether the particular idea is a good or a bad one. Thus even a failure is exciting, and most of my ideas have of course been wrong."[24]

The more things you try, the faster you will find out what doesn't work. When you use that information to self-correct, you'll eventually arrive at the right answer—that is, the one that works in solving the problem.

Better Thoughts, Better Outcomes

Chef René Redzepi consistently pushes the boundaries of what's acceptable in the world of haute cuisine. He believes that extreme constraints are the secret to innovation, so his restaurant uses only ingredients native to Nordic countries. Since the growing season is short, his team often forages for the ingredients in their dishes.

He's famous for what he calls "Trash Cooking," basically using ingredients others wouldn't touch, including fried fish scales, lamb brains, dried spruce and fir needles, and other oddities. "The best discoveries are hidden somewhere in insanity," he says.[25] What might happen, for instance, if you roasted cauliflower like poultry, or prepared carrots like beef, or made a dessert from cucumber? As it turns out, people will ask for more.

Of course, some ideas don't work. In one year, for instance, he and his team produced over one hundred new successful recipes—but many more than that which were ultimately rejected.[26]

What always works is the creative method itself—deconstructing and recombining ingredients, blending and adapting techniques, pairing and marrying ideas that others would reject or might never imagine to begin with. As a result, *TIME* magazine declared Redzepi a "God of Food," he's been awarded three Michelin stars, and his Copenhagen restaurant, Noma, has been named World's Best Restaurant four times.

What accounts for this relentless innovation? Redzepi sums it up in an entry from his personal journal: "Creativity is the ability to store the special moments, big or small, that occur throughout your life, then being able to see how they connect to the moment you're in. When past and present merge, something new happens."[27]

Progress never results from obvious answers or commonsense practices. Such things are invaluable, to be sure. But their purpose is to maintain business as usual or, at best, to return

Progress never results from obvious answers or commonsense practices.

to normal. There is a vast difference between producing greater efficiency and driving real progress.

To solve the problems you face, you need the kind of creativity Redzepi describes: the ability to see new connections between your past experience and your current reality. That involves forging new neural pathways in your brain by pushing yourself beyond your current thinking, the prevailing view, and even common sense. Sometimes, it requires you to entertain thoughts that seem extreme, unworkable, or even crazy.

When you do, your mind will begin to generate new ideas. Your default ways of thinking will be replaced by more compelling and empowering stories. Your thoughts, emotions, and actions will be reshaped in the process. And you'll begin to experience results in your life, relationships, and business that had seemed previously unattainable.

We cannot urge you strongly enough to open your mind, set aside your limiting thoughts, and explore new experiences and ideas that will generate real transformation in your life.

There is one limit to your thinking, however, that you cannot change on your own. There are thoughts that your mind is simply incapable of creating. To gain access to them, you'll need to get inside the head of someone else. In the next chapter, we'll tell you how to leverage the thought power of other people to generate solutions to your most pressing problems.

NINE

More Brains Are Better Than One

In 1905, while working in a German patent office, Albert Einstein came up with a new explanation for how light traveled, a discovery that eventually landed him a Nobel Prize in Physics. That same year, he also published his theory of special relativity and his famous formula $E=mc^2$.

And that wasn't all. Over the span of a few months, the unknown Einstein published several of the most significant papers in the history of science. He was just twenty-six years old but well on his way to becoming one of the greatest scientists of the twentieth century and certainly the most recognizable.

Einstein became one of very few scientists—along with maybe Newton, Darwin, and Tesla—to become a pop-culture icon. Thousands mobbed a theater in New York in 1930 to see a movie about his theory of relativity.[1]

"He was the embodiment of pure intellect," said *TIME* magazine when it named him Person of the Century in 1999, "the genius among geniuses who discovered, merely by thinking about it, that the universe was not as it seemed."[2] But as amazing as Einstein's mind truly was, there's more to the story than gigantic intellect and solitary breakthroughs.

Surprisingly, Einstein was mostly ignored by fellow scientists in his final decades. One colleague described him as a "landmark but not a beacon."[3] He was recognized for his past achievements but failed to attract new interest in his work.

"I am generally regarded as a sort of petrified object," Einstein wrote to a friend.[4] He had stagnated. How? He stopped listening to others.

Consider this statement from one of Einstein's professors back when he was an undergrad in Zurich. "Einstein," he said, "you have one great fault. You do not let yourself be told anything."[5] That fault stayed with him.

Einstein's self-certainty was an asset at first, but it eventually meant he was closed to new ideas, and as the field of quantum mechanics outpaced his theories, Einstein found himself pushed to the sidelines.[6] As it turns out, even the geniuses among us cannot think enough new thoughts to sustain innovation over a lifetime. To solve the most urgent problems we face, we must find a way to leverage the thinking of others.

I (MEGAN) WOULD LIKE TO SAY that I learned from Einstein's example when rewriting my story about my limitations as a public speaker. Truth is, I knew I'd gone as far as I could by myself. I needed the guidance, coaching, and expertise of others.

I had begun my journey using some of the techniques previously mentioned. I took ownership of my thoughts by writing affirmations on a legal pad, describing the possibilities I saw for myself in vivid detail. I read this aloud every single day for several weeks while drying my hair. I was telling a new story, reprogramming my brain.

That was a start, but it wasn't enough. My Narrator was underequipped to help me speak before a crowd. To begin with, it had been working against me for years. I didn't have the kind of experiences onstage that would lead me to believe I could simply walk out and make a dazzling presentation to a packed house. Owning my new identity did not address the gaps in my knowledge and skill. I needed help to learn how to speak in public and develop the ability to do it.

I contacted a therapist who specializes in anxiety for speaking. I talked to my doctor about anxiety medication. Though I didn't wind up using the medication, understanding how anxiety was affecting my brain and knowing that I could do something about it was a tremendous help.

Next, I turned to the experts on our content team to help me write a speech—something I'd never done before for obvious reasons. My sister Mary, a life coach, helped me further master my mindset and replace limiting beliefs with possibility-rich ideas.

Finally, as I mentioned, I hired my good friend Michele Cushatt, who happens to be one of the most sought-after speaking coaches in the country, to guide me through the process of developing and delivering my first keynote address.

These people became my team. Remember what we said in chapter 3 about how the brain tells stories. It works with whatever we've *earned* through our own experience or *learned* from others. If we find our own personal experience and knowledge insufficient, we can get what we need from others. We can benefit from the unique neural connections in their heads. Often, this is a necessary element in helping our Narrator to imagine better stories.

Outside Input

Effective leadership involves a commitment to personal growth and development, and that requires outside input. Writing about this for *Harvard Business Review*, Kenneth Mikkelsen and Harold Jarche say, "Leaders must get comfortable with living in a state of continual *becoming*, a perpetual beta mode."[7] Leaders who stay on top do so by being receptive and able to learn.

It's difficult to critique your own thinking. You have only your experience and viewpoint to rely on. Meanwhile, other people know things you don't. Their unique experience and knowledge enable them to see things you can't see—things that might be the difference between hitting a wall or achieving your goals. In the case of Einstein, it was the difference between irrelevance and making an ongoing contribution to a field that might have benefited from his insight.

Because we all have different starting points and experiences, our assumptions vary and diverge, sometimes radically. Others are able to conceive of ideas that would, quite literally, never occur to us. Their mental model of the world and its possibilities is different from ours.

The good news is, while in the past, leaders used to refuse coaching because it seemed remedial, that perspective seems to be fading. Leaders now look to coaches for insight on conflict management, team building, delegation, and other challenges. The right coach, consultant, or counselor can diagnose flaws in your thinking quickly and thoroughly. They can also improve your performance through expert critique.

Psychologist Anders Ericsson's study of outstanding performers in sports, music, chess, and other disciplines validates this concept. Ericsson's findings, published in the book *Peak*, have been popularized in the idea of the "10,000-Hour Rule," which states that 10,000 hours of practice are required to gain mastery in any pursuit.

But that's not precisely what Ericsson found. Practice alone is not enough to produce results. You can do something wrong ten thousand times.

Rather, guided practice produces progress. In other words, athletes, musicians, and even doctors who received specific feedback from a coach to correct their mistakes were the ones who benefited from the long hours of experience. Without feedback, growth slows, or even stops altogether.[8]

A leader must continually grow and develop into the kind of leader required for the next place they're going. Otherwise, their organization will outgrow them or, worse, get stuck behind them and stagnate. To keep your team in growth mode, you must be leading the way in your development. And to do that, you need outside help.

Earlier, I (Michael) mentioned the executive coach who challenged my thinking with a bold question: "What is it about your leadership that led to this outcome?" That moment perfectly encapsulates what we're talking about here. I need other people to help me discover insights I can't generate on my own. My thinking is always bound by the limits of my experience, community, and imagination.

Though my brain is capable of making over 100 trillion neural connections, it probably won't. Even after more than four decades in business, marriage, and parenting, I just don't have that much knowledge and experience. There are thoughts I simply won't arrive at on my own. That's why I've consistently made use of coaches, counselors, and teachers throughout my life. Still do. Always will.

And it's why I (Megan) never miss a coaching session, even though my schedule as CEO, wife, and mom is extremely busy. We need other people to help us think new thoughts. And it's worth paying for the benefit of more brains than your own.

OF COURSE, YOU DON'T ALWAYS have to pay for expert advice. Thanks to the internet, and even the humble public library, the thoughts of many of the most innovative thinkers of all time are just a click or browse away.

That instant availability of knowledge, though, has created an interesting paradox. On the one hand, we have more information at our fingertips than ever before. On the other hand, we have become more siloed, listening more and more to people who see the world as we do.[9]

It is impossible to interrogate a story from the inside of an echo chamber. But when you take in books, articles, podcasts, and other media produced by people who are different from you—who perhaps even tell a different story about the world— you gain the opportunity to ask new questions.

You may change your story, or you may not. In either case, you'll be better informed and in a stronger position to check your assumptions.

Borrowing other people's thoughts is essentially what we do every time we read a book, listen to a podcast, watch a video, or hold a conversation. We upload stories created by other people into our own minds. There we can interrogate them, harvest the meaningful concepts and connections, and mix them into our own thinking. By doing so, we are essentially mining the experience and insight of others in search of gold.

Find Your Long Hallway

Bell Labs was the most prolific scientific research site in the world for many years. It was the research and development arm of AT&T, and it gave us the transistor, the calculator, direct long-distance dialing, fiber optics, lasers, the first cellular phone systems, and much more.

One reason the engineers there were so productive is that the laboratory spaces opened onto a central hallway over two hundred yards long. Employees were instructed to keep their doors open as a way to generate the free flow of ideas.

Along that corridor, people working on a variety of different problems would bump into one another every day. That produced thousands of spontaneous conversations across department lines. It could be argued that more breakthroughs were made in that one hallway than in all the lab spaces combined.[10]

Though they didn't invent it, the engineers at Bell Labs were making use of what's called *lateral thinking*. This refers to the practice of thinking in areas that are adjacent or parallel to the problem you're working on. Often, that takes place in unstructured contexts—such as hallway conversations—where people with different skill sets, knowledge, or experience can share their input on a problem not directly related to their own work.

As longtime conference leaders, we've known for years that the most imaginative and productive exchanges at our events take place in the margins. Plenary sessions and workshops are usually packed with great speakers who download a ton of information. That's always interesting, but the real action happens during the breaks. When attendees mingle over coffee, they have the opportunity to engage in lateral thinking. That's when the creative sparks fly.

This is also why we always include time for peer interaction during our company's coaching events. Invariably, attendees report that their breakthrough moments emerge during these spontaneous peer-to-peer interactions.

If you don't have an opportunity for peer mentoring in some existing context, you can create your own. That's essentially what I (Michael) did when I was CEO at Thomas Nelson. I knew I needed peer interaction for sharing ideas and generating new ones.

This was before mastermind groups and peer coaching came on the scene. I decided to meet once a quarter with three other public company CEOs in the Nashville area. One member of the group would come prepared with an idea or content to briefly present, then we'd dive into discussion. I always came away with more fresh ideas than I walked in with. It was enormously helpful.

Ask an Outsider

The *invisible obvious* is a term coined by psychological researcher Jan Smedslund to describe the cultural blindness that prevents people in a given context from seeing what is obvious to outsiders.[11] What we call "common sense" is common only because we have a shared understanding of the world, a common culture. Somebody else's common sense may not be the same as yours.[12]

Of course we smile when introduced to someone, tip restaurant servers, and shower daily. Doesn't everyone? No, they don't. These practices are so thoroughly embedded in our reality that we seldom notice them. Yet they consistently puzzle people from other cultures. They're invisible to us but obvious to everyone else.

We all have cultural blind spots that prevent us from seeing connections that might be obvious to others. That's true whether the culture is national, ethnic, regional, corporate, or even familial. Few of us can see, let alone think, beyond the confines of our own reality.

As we said earlier, there are thoughts you cannot think, questions you cannot ask, and conclusions you cannot draw because they simply wouldn't occur to you. To gain access to them, you need to collaborate with people whose most basic stories are different from your own. You need diverse inputs.

There's a strong business case to be made for this. Writing in *MIT Sloan Management Review*, professors Jean-Louis Barsoux, Cyril Bouquet, and Michael Wade point to several studies where outsider perspectives were critical for creative breakthroughs. "[A] study of 166 problem-solving contests posted on the InnoCentive innovation platform found that the winning entries were more likely to have come from 'unexpected contributors' whose areas of expertise were foreign to the focal field of inquiry," they write.[13]

Another study tested how in-line skaters, roofers, and carpenters would improve kneepads, safety belts, and respiratory masks. One group of participants had expert knowledge for each item in the mix: the skaters knew the kneepads, the roofers knew the safety belts, and the carpenters knew the masks.

There are thoughts
you cannot think,
questions you cannot
ask, and conclusions
you cannot draw
because they simply
wouldn't occur to you.

Surprisingly, the best improvements came from those who were nonexperts in the items.

"Confirming this advantage of marginality," write Barsoux and his colleagues, "a separate crowdsourcing study revealed that industry outsiders were more likely than insiders to come up with breakthrough solutions to relatively complex and intractable R&D problems."[14]

To humanize these findings, the authors point to the case of pioneering eye surgeon and inventor Dr. Patricia Bath. Bath's career represents an impressive string of firsts, including being the first African American woman to obtain a medical patent, stemming from her creation of laserphaco cataract surgery. Despite the promise of her invention, Bath rarely received support or encouragement from peers. Ironically, their insider status blinded them to her discovery.

Bath pushed ahead regardless and revolutionized eye care, ultimately securing several patents and industry recognition. "Her technique remains in use worldwide," write Barsoux and his colleagues.[15]

Studies and stories such as these highlight what University of Michigan professor Scott Page refers to as "the diversity bonus." The challenges faced in today's economy—think ideation, IT, manufacturing, supply chain, commerce—are often complex and well beyond the scope of any one individual or even singular disciplines. Leaders and teams need a diversity of backgrounds and expertise and the ability to bridge divides if they are to arrive at integrative solutions.[16]

There are less formal ways of gaining insight from a diversity of perspectives. For example, asking for input from an acquaintance of a different background or ethnicity, talking with coworkers in different roles or specialties, attending conferences that are not directly related to your work, or even reading international authors. The starting point is to ask, "Who might have a different perspective on this problem than I do?"

Go back to the example of brainstorming from the prior chapter. When we're cramped for time, we generate relevant ideas that we can all easily agree on. But they're usually nothing to write home about. Not what we're looking for when it comes to innovation. The magic comes when someone fires an idea out of left field. Maybe it's brilliant; maybe it's terrible. But it's finally something worth batting around, maybe even arguing about. When that happens, new and different ideas start bubbling up in reaction— possibilities no one would have landed on if unprovoked.

All of this can be challenging, and that's the point. If you are unwilling to invite challenges to your current way of seeing reality, you'll be unlikely to come up with new and better ideas. Ideas that are generated more often in the coming together of diverse, even disagreeable, opinions.

You Can't Argue with Results

A widely cited bit of folk wisdom goes something like this: Learn from the mistakes of others; you can't live long enough to make them all yourself. We can honestly say that some of the greatest achievements in our professional lives and business have been a direct result of leveraging the thinking of others through coaching, reading, peer mentoring, and customer feedback.

Thinking with other people has dramatically shaped our business and our lives. Full Focus would look much different today, and have a lesser impact, if we had not been willing to consult with others, take advice, and learn from everyone, from our customers to our coaches and employees.

Personally, we've seen the benefits as well. In every domain of life, including our relationships, health, and personal finances, we've made the greatest strides when actively engaging others in examining our thinking and identifying solutions.

It also helped me (Megan) to train my Narrator to tell better stories when it came to public speaking. Just a few months after determining I needed to face my fear, after sending that text to Michele, and after my team came and asked me to keynote, I stepped onstage and did it.

I stood before a packed auditorium at our Achieve conference and delivered my talk. I paced the stage, spoke with force and conviction, clicked through my slides, and stuck the landing—all with audience laughter in the right spots. It went flawlessly, which, given how hard I had avoided speaking, seems actually funny in retrospect.

Joel said I betrayed no hint of anxiety, which was gratifying. My dad—Mr. Professional Speaker—said that he was proud and that he couldn't have done better himself. I know he could, but, man, it felt good to hear him say it. Even better were the comments, emails, and texts from conferees thanking me for sharing a message that proved transformational in their lives.

None of that would have been possible if I had simply said, "I'm a public speaker," and written it on a vision board. To bring that idea to life, I had to leverage knowledge and expertise that I couldn't access on my own. I needed other people.

> If the only thoughts you're willing to think are the ones you currently have, then the only results you'll get are the ones you're getting.

If the only thoughts you're willing to think are the ones you currently have, then the only results you'll get are the ones you're getting. This doesn't mean you are incapable of solving problems on your own. In fact, thinking is a kind of superpower for humans. All day, every day, whether you're awake or asleep, your brain is busy solving problems. What it does mean, as we've seen in this chapter, is that you can improve your results if you include more superheroes like you in the mix.

In the next chapter, we'll explore how you can upgrade your superpower so it works even better than it does now.

TEN

Let Your Mind Run

One evening I (Michael) was working on a writing project, and the words were not coming easily. I'd written several drafts, yet nothing seemed right. It just wouldn't come together. The achiever in me did not want to admit defeat, so I gamely began another draft sometime around eleven o'clock.

Sensing my anxiety, my wife, Gail, asked what I was working on. "It's a presentation for tomorrow's meeting. I can't seem to get a handle on it, but I've got to deliver it at 10:00 a.m."

"Michael," she said kindly but firmly, "just go to bed. It will all work out in the morning." I doubted that, but I also sensed there would be no more progress that night. I closed my computer and hit the sack.

Sure enough, at six o'clock the next morning I opened my laptop and discovered that Gail had been right. The ideas began to flow. I banged out the rest of my presentation in about twenty minutes.

That phenomenon is not uncommon. You've probably experienced something like it yourself. Imaginative thinking is a painstakingly slow process, and very frustrating. Sometimes it seems that the more we focus on a problem, the harder it is to find a solution. Yet when we take a walk, get a bite to eat, or go to sleep, we find that the elusive answers are right there waiting for us.

Why does that happen so often? And how can we make that process more predictable?

PHILOSOPHER OF SCIENCE Thomas Kuhn, author of the landmark book *The Structure of Scientific Revolution*, relates an experience remarkably like the one just mentioned. While reading Aristotle's work on physics, Kuhn was surprised that Aristotle's work, the foundation for our understanding of the universe, seemed riddled with logical errors. Wondering how to reconcile these ideas, Kuhn says:

> I continued to puzzle over the text. . . . I was sitting at my desk with the text of Aristotle's *Physics* open in front of me and with a four-colored pencil in my hand. Looking up, I gazed abstractedly out the window of my room—the visual image is one I still retain. Suddenly the fragments in my head sorted themselves out in a new way, and fell into place together.[1]

"The fragments in my head sorted themselves out in a new way"—what a powerful picture of how our minds can help us reformulate our thoughts.

Kuhn possessed the same old concepts, but his subconscious recombined them in new ways. His brain was making new connections, even when it appeared to be doing nothing. That resulted in an *aha* moment in which the solution seemed to appear out of nowhere. In fact, the brain had been laying the groundwork for that insight for some time.

When we imagine or reimagine a story, we're not creating something entirely new. We're mostly finding new relationships between the concepts and contexts we already possess. Neuroscientist György Buzsáki says that when we face something new, the brain will try to match it to existing neural pathways—thoughts or stories. If needed, it will add to or delete connections from the existing structure to make sense of the situation.[2]

"New ideas, solutions, and art forms are not created in a vacuum," confirms Elkhonon Goldberg. "To a very large extent, they arise as novel configurations of the elements of previously formed ideas, solutions, and forms."[3]

Remember when we said that every idea is formed by a particular assembly of neurons in your brain? Each one takes a specific configuration or shape. Thinking new thoughts involves rearranging the connections or making new ones. You arrive at new thoughts by making novel connections between the ideas and experiences you already have.

When actively solving problems, we rely heavily on the brain's prefrontal cortex. This is the part we use for conscious thought, and it excels at this reassembly process. It likes to recombine bits of information to create something new, sort of like building an airplane from the LEGO blocks that used to be a house.[4]

But there's more to your brain, much more. And your brain can engage in this sorting process whether you're thinking about it or not. To move beyond your default ways of thinking, especially when you are stuck on a problem, you'll need to enlist the vast network of neurons that functions largely outside your conscious thought.

Your Other Brain

We usually think of *brainpower* as our ability to do intense, focused thinking about an idea or problem. Yet your brain works at the subconscious level too. Because it takes advantage of the vast network of synapses not used for conscious thinking, subconscious thought often provides breakthrough solutions that elude the conscious mind.

If your conscious thoughts are like a hare, quick and deliberate but easily tired, your subconscious thoughts are like a tortoise, slow and plodding but relentlessly effective.

Scientists have discovered that the brain has many more structures than previously thought, and those structures do more than was previously known.[5] For example, when thinking about a problem, the left side of the brain makes the obvious connections to more relevant solutions. Meanwhile, the right side searches for more novel answers. To be precise, these novel solutions are generated from increased neural activity in a bit of brain tissue located above the right ear, the right anterior superior temporal gyrus.[6] (Don't worry. That won't be on the test.)

So it is true that the left hemisphere of the brain is better wired for analytical thought while the right hemisphere is more likely to range freely, allowing for more innovative thought. Yet in reality, the two types of thinking are more associated with neural networks or modes than with specific regions.[7]

There are two networks (or modes) of neurons within your brain. The *executive network* (or mode) is guided by you, your conscious self. It thinks about what you tell it to. This is the top-down, left hemisphere–dominated network that loves analysis, order, familiar patterns, and predictability.

The *default network* (or mode) is self-directed. This is the bottom-up, right hemisphere–dominant network that loves novelty and creativity and operates largely in your subconscious.[8] Of course you don't really have two separate brains. These are two neural networks within your brain that operate in different ways.

To find creative solutions to your problems you need to get this second part of the brain into action. This vast network of slower-firing neurons is highly adaptable. It can be endlessly reconfigured to provide new thoughts and connections.[9] Sure, this takes longer than using conscious thought, but it's highly effective.

WHEN WORKING on *The Last Supper*, Leonardo da Vinci was known to quit working unexpectedly. He would sometimes spend half a day doing nothing, lost in his own thoughts. His patron wasn't thrilled by that. He wanted him to keep his tools in hand, just like the gardener working outside. But da Vinci convinced him otherwise. His argument, according to Renaissance historian Giorgio Vasari, was this:

> The greatest geniuses sometimes accomplish more when they work less, since they are searching for inventions in their minds, and forming those perfect ideas which their hands then express and reproduce from what they previously conceived with their intellect.[10]

In other words, not working was still working. How?

It's right there in Vasari's phrases "searching for inventions" and "forming those perfect ideas." While da Vinci painted, brush in hand, he executed his plan, expressing and reproducing what he had imagined. But first he had to imagine it. That required stepping away from the canvas to let his mind run, riffling through his mental inventory of shape and color.

That effort of conscious thought exposed challenges and problems with his approach, some of which stopped him in his tracks. But as he puzzled away, daydreamed, or meandered off to do other tasks, his unconscious mind was free to keep searching and forming.

It might have taken hours, but when the right idea fell into place, da Vinci was able to pick up his brushes and begin again. The key takeaway in the story is that he—or at least part of him—was working the whole time.

The default network employs those little "daemons" we mentioned in chapter 2. Like the Narrator, they scour experiences, memories, stories, concepts, and connections, all while you eat, sleep, or take a shower. During these seemingly mindless activities, your subconscious is clicking through the vast collection of thoughts buried deep in your mind. It tries one connection, then another, and another, and another, looking for one that will make better sense of your reality. When it finds one, "Eureka!" It elevates the thought to your conscious mind.

> Imaginative insights are produced by your subconscious mind when given the right opportunity to think.

These serendipitous insights are not the product of focused thought or of some mysterious creative gift. And they don't depend on luck. Imaginative insights are produced by your subconscious mind when given the right opportunity to think.

On/Off

The executive network and the default network don't operate at precisely the same time. They seesaw back and forth. When we are focusing and working hard on a project, our executive control is in play. When we disengage from a task, our default mode takes over.

"When your mind is at rest, what it is really doing is bouncing thoughts back and forth," says neuroscientist Nancy Coover Andreasen. "Your association cortices are always running in the background, but when you are not focused on some task—for example, when you are doing something mindless, like driving—that's when your mind is most free to roam. That's why that is when you most actively create new ideas."[11] In the language of computer science, these are the operations your brain runs in the background.

When you have an *aha* moment, it's usually the result of synergistic interaction between the two networks. So to boost your creativity, it's important to alternate between the two. You need periods of focus on a problem, and periods of letting your conscious mind rest.[12]

Here's why that works so well. When you are actively thinking about a problem, your executive network calls up the relevant concepts to toy around with. When you switch to default mode, your brain continues that process. But get this: Those concepts, represented by neural dots in your brain, exist in different networks in your default mode! That means your brain is using different pathways to connect the same set of dots.[13]

Think of your executive network like an interstate highway. Traffic moves fast, and it's the easiest way to get from point A to point B. Imagine traveling to a specific destination on that highway, say Interstate 70. What happens if there's a traffic jam or a road closure? What if you *can't* get from A to B on I-70? It's no problem, because point B is also accessible via State Road 38, US 36, Jonesboro Pike, County Road 300, State Street, and Pendleton Avenue. There are any number of other ways to get there. It'll just take you a bit longer.

Free from the single-track thinking of the executive network, the default mode looks for all sorts of solutions that might never occur to your conscious mind. That takes a bit of time, but it's almost certain to produce a breakthrough if given enough time and space.

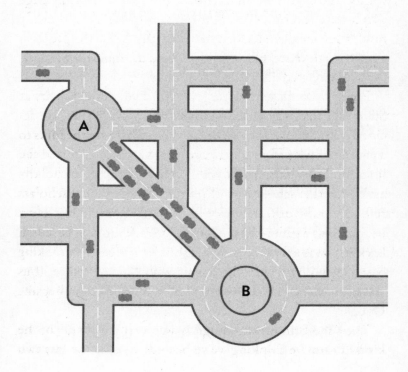

Can you shortcut the process? Sometimes. To be effective in problem-solving, your default network does best when primed with a period of deliberate thought.[14] The reason is simple: it finds more solutions when it knows what it's looking for. Conscious, executive thought narrows the focus so the default network has a good starting point.

It's a bit like searching online. In the early days of the internet, searching was like rooting around in a file cabinet. For example, to find something on Yahoo! in the mid-1990s, you began with a list of category links, then clicked on one to open a list of sub links, and so on. It was cumbersome and tedious.

The next generation of search engines was based on keywords. The engine would scour the internet to find any page that listed the term. A search for "boxers" would produce any result from men's underwear to Muhammad Ali. The problem there was relevance. How could you find the most *useful* pages, those that related directly to your inquiry?

Enter Larry Page and Sergey Brin, two grad students at Stanford University. Based on advice from a professor, Page decided to study backlinks on the internet. These are the links to a particular page from other pages. Page and Brin realized the links on the web compared roughly to citations of a scholarly article in other scholarly works; the more times other scholars refer to your work, the more important or relevant it must be. This was a game-changing insight. Page ranking based on backlinks was a far more reliable search method than ranking based solely on keywords because it factored in relevance. Thus was born the search algorithm BackRub, which later became Google.[15]

The Page-Brin breakthrough is a powerful example of the kind of creative thinking we've been discussing the last two chapters. It's also a picture of what your brain is doing on the inside all the time. It's "searching for inventions," to employ Giorgio Vasari's phrase.

You can preprogram the work of your default network by spending some time thinking about the idea or problem you're working on. Those conscious thoughts become the backlinks in your default mode's search algorithm. They prime your default network to look for specific, relevant connections, which makes it more likely that it will find them.

To get more creative with a problem, think about it and then stop for a bit. Put your brain into default mode and let it work on its own. As we'll see next, one way to amplify your results over time is to include regular periods of exercise and rest.

Optimize Your Brain

In 2009, researchers studied 1,271 schoolchildren in grades five through nine to determine the effect of regular exercise on learning. They discovered kids who had more than four hours of scheduled exercise per week scored significantly higher on standardized tests.[16] You may have noticed that your ability to think, solve problems, or remember details improves after a brisk walk or an invigorating workout.

But why? The answer has to do with brain chemistry. The synapses in the brain are a mix of electrical and chemical properties. Every synapse takes electrical current, converts it to a chemical, then returns it to electrical current. Those chemicals, called *neurotransmitters*, are the body's messengers. They transmit the electrical signal from one nerve cell to another, or to other types of cells.

As it turns out, exercise stimulates the production of the neurotransmitters serotonin, norepinephrine, and endorphins. Muscle action also produces proteins that travel through the bloodstream and into the brain, where they "play pivotal roles in the mechanisms of our highest thought processes," according to professor of psychiatry John Ratey.[17] In other words, exercise is good for your brain. It helps you think.

That's not all. Stress has an equal but adverse effect. It erodes the connections between nerve cells and can even shrink certain areas of the brain.[18] That may explain why, after thinking about a problem for too long and becoming stressed about your inability to solve it, you may be left feeling "brain dead."

As Ratey puts it, "the brain responds like muscles do, growing with use, withering with inactivity." And physical exercise produces the key chemicals that enhance brain function and promote brain cell growth.

In fact, Ratey refers to a particular chemical, the brain-derived neurotrophic factor (BDNF), as "Miracle-Gro" for the brain because it enables learning and aids the growth of new brain cells. BDNF is held in reserve pools near the synapses and is released during exercise.[19]

All of this means your brain functions much more robustly after exercise than before. The experience of taking a bike ride or lifting weights and then feeling that your mind was alive with new ideas is not a fluke. To state the obvious, your brain and body are intimately connected. When your body is operating at an optimal level, your brain will too.

To activate your mind, activate your body. As demonstrated by countless studies, consistent exercise can have a dramatic effect on your ability to learn new concepts, recall information, and solve problems.

Even a brief walk outside can improve your cognitive function. Puzzling over that intractable problem for another hour
might actually prevent you from finding a solution. Do like
da Vinci and disengage. It might be better to supercharge
your brain with a brisk walk, then let your default network
take over.

BEING RELAXED AND PLAYFUL in your approach to a
problem also aids subconscious thought. You can set yourself
up for what will later appear to be serendipitous discoveries by
not thinking directly about the problem but approaching it
with this seemingly counterintuitive mindset.[20]

Rest, play, and idleness are not unproductive activities in
terms of problem-solving. They're vital practices for mental hy-
giene. They relieve stress, rest your mind, and allow it to operate
in its deeper, slower default mode.

Sleep matters too. Research indicates that sleep has a direct impact on cognitive function, especially in the ability
to learn and remember. According to neuroscientist Matthew Walker, when you are asleep, your default network is
still very much at work. This is especially true when you're
in dreamland, the REM sleep that generally occurs later in
your sleep cycle, toward morning. Your brain is busy sorting,
processing, and making sense of your memories.[21] This is precisely the meaning-making process we learned about in chapter 2, whereby your brain forms stories by connecting your
experiences.

Not surprisingly, lack of sleep produces the opposite effect:
brain fog, poor judgment, and difficulty remembering. Experts

recommend a minimum of seven hours of sleep per night to keep body and brain functioning at optimal levels.

Naps also put the brain into default mode, which is one reason I (Michael) have been an advocate for taking a midday nap for many years. Twenty to thirty minutes of shut-eye after lunch makes my mind sharper and thoughts clearer.

Naturally, that breakthrough I had on my writing project came after a good night's sleep. When my Narrator and I finally called it quits and went to sleep, my default network went to work. Whether by simply practicing a hobby, going to sleep, or just thinking about something else for a while, engaging your default mode may be the most productive thing you do today.

Not All Who Wander Are Lost

Joel and I (Megan) drove to Rochester, Minnesota, and back to Nashville, Tennessee, awhile back. We planned to fly, but we realized a scheduling snafu about an hour too late. Joel, who loves driving, suggested we take the truck instead. I wasn't excited about it, but we didn't have many options. So off we went.

The round-trip drive takes about twenty-four hours, which gave us a long time for thought and conversation. The GPS ensured that our vehicle never veered off course, but there was no programmed route for our discussion. It wandered from vacation to parenting to work, back to parenting, then books, friends, music, and finally to the design of a new product we'd been working on before the trip. By the time we pulled into the driveway back home, we'd outlined the key features and—with the help of the rest of the team—the product was released several weeks later.

How on earth did we get from "Gosh, there's a lot of corn between here and home" to "I think we can launch next quarter"? There certainly was no straight line connecting those dots. But there was a common thread.

Like a series of stepping-stones, each element of our meandering conversation led us one step closer to the discoveries that would make our idea successful. There was no huge leap from simply driving to conceiving a product launch. It was a series of small steps. Frankly, if Joel had said, "Hey, let's spend the next eight hours talking about work," it wouldn't have happened. Yet taking one small step at a time, we were able to arrive at a fresh, exciting new idea.

That's generally how problem-solving works, especially when the default mode is engaged. Nearby connections become the stepping-stones of great discoveries.

This is what Steven Johnson has referred to as the "adjacent possible," borrowing a phrase from scientist Stuart Kauffman. Making a crazy leap from one idea into another usually doesn't happen; instead, we nudge ourselves there by degrees, entertaining possibilities close to what we already regard as true. "The strange and beautiful truth about the adjacent possible is that its boundaries grow as you explore those boundaries," says Johnson. "Each new combination ushers new combinations into the adjacent possible."[22] That's why even "wrong" answers are sometimes right, because they can edge you closer to something that will prove effective.

Your default network excels at this purposeful meandering. Wandering thoughts do not signal a disengaged mind. A certain amount of mind-wandering may be required to take the small steps that produce wildly creative solutions.

A certain amount of mind-wandering may be required to take the small steps that produce wildly creative solutions.

FORMING NEW CONNECTIONS is a mental process that happens, to a large degree, in the subconscious. While there are techniques for fostering those discoveries, the process cannot be rushed. Reimagining your stories requires persistence. But it doesn't have to be front and center in your mind, twenty-four hours a day. That's why da Vinci could put down his paint and brush and still make progress—his mind was at work, even when he wasn't.

You already have all or most of the concepts. These are the experiences and ideas that you're trying to make sense of. You know the possible variables in context. All of that was laid out in your interrogation phase. Now you've got to try different combinations, looking for new ways to make meaning from the same bits of material. It's a sorting problem. And sometimes what you need, in order to find breakthrough in that sorting and recombining work, is to step away and let your mind wander.

Most of us have had the experience of serendipitous discovery at some point. A good night's sleep, a shower, or a walk in the park seems to be just the thing to spark that extra bit of creative insight. Now that you know about your brain's vast default network and how it functions, you're better prepared to engage your subconscious mind as an ally in problem-solving. As you do, you'll experience those *aha* moments with greater regularity and predictability. It's not a matter of luck or magic. This is simply how your brain works. So take a break every now and then, and let your brain do what it does best.

ACTION

Return to the story you've been working on in your Full Focus Self-Coacher (fullfocus.co/self-coacher). Do you see how you could use the details to tell a better story?

What new details and insights could you include? Who could you consult? Now that you've started working on the problem in your conscious mind, what might happen if you slept on it, or went for a walk?

Take what you've learned and imagine a different, more helpful story.

WHAT WE KNOW NOW

▶ Asking possibility questions allows for exploration and discovery, which lie at the heart of imagination.

▶ The way to spark a breakthrough sometimes is to dial your thinking up to "crazy," then pull it back a notch.

▶ Creativity occurs at the intersection of novelty and relevance.

▶ To gain access to thoughts you cannot think, questions you cannot ask, and conclusions you cannot draw because they simply wouldn't occur to you, you need to collaborate with people whose most basic stories are different from your own.

▶ To get more creative with a problem, stop thinking about it.

How does that relate to the story we've been telling since the beginning of the book?

▶ The Narrator uses everything we've earned or learned in the past to help us reach our goals in the future.

▶ It's usually helpful, though sometimes it steers us wrong.

▶ We need to learn to challenge our Narrator when we feel stuck or want to improve the results we're experiencing.

▶ We can do that by interrogating the stories we tell and then imagining something better.

▶ Over time we can train the Narrator to tell better, more helpful stories.

ELEVEN

Making the Narrator Your Ally

When she was a child, René Banglesdorf's father communicated a thought to her that would become a guiding force in her life. "René," he said, "you can do whatever you set your mind to." And she believed that for a long time. She did well in school and was popular with her friends. Throughout high school and into college, René was a high achiever.

Fast-forward twenty years. After an unplanned pregnancy, René had dropped out of college to start a family. Her husband, Curt, worked as a broker for the sale of private aircraft. He asked her to help with marketing the business, so she reentered the workforce.

After a few years, the duo started their own company as equal partners. René's work in branding the company, defining their offer to the customer, and identifying new clients produced immediate results. She became known within the industry.

"Yet I always saw myself as a woman first," she said, "a woman in a male-dominated industry. I was pretty good at hanging out with the guys and not being easily offended at things that they said, even when perhaps I should have been."

The little girl who believed she could succeed at anything had become a highly competent woman, but one who saw herself as a college dropout, an outsider in a male-dominated world.

Then something clicked.

"I was at a conference in London," René explains, "and I was hanging out on the sidelines with a couple of my guys, really more my husband's friends than mine. And I thought, *Why am I standing here on the outskirts of this conversation? I'm not really even part of this.*"

That moment of insight became the catalyst for rethinking her assumptions about her place in the world.

"I decided to start seeking out other women," she said, "to build a tribe of my own. And so I walked away from those guys and started introducing myself to other women. That changed something for me. I began to see my identity as a woman as an advantage. Instead of trying to fit in, I decided to embrace standing out."

That moment of discovery changed everything for René. She now says, "I want to make a difference, not just in the industry but as a woman in the industry, for women in the industry."

René became even more purposeful in her work. When regulatory matters made it advantageous for René to replace Curt as leader of the firm, she agreed. Before long, her elevated profile and message of empowerment for women gained traction.

She was invited to participate on corporate and nonprofit boards and to speak in settings that would not have been available to her before. She was also appointed to an FAA Women in Aviation Advisory Board to make recommendations to the FAA and US Congress to increase the number of women in aviation. "I've had a number of women say, 'Thank you so much for stepping up. You're a role model to me.'" This includes her daughter, who is a professional pilot.

RENÉ'S STORY IS INSPIRING. It also traces the evolution of her Narrator throughout her life. Remember that the Narrator connects our experiences and memories to form a story for all the situations we face. In the beginning, the Narrator had one primary source to work with—René's father and his relentless encouragement. That story propelled her to a standout career in high school and a great start in college.

After leaving college to start a family, a decision René does not regret, her Narrator adopted a new theme: "René is a mom who has no professional role." Not surprisingly, she reentered the business world timidly. Although her contributions were outstanding, she still saw herself as an outsider.

Then came the *aha* moment, the incident at the industry conference when she suddenly realized that being a woman and an industry outsider were advantages, not hindrances. That thought did not arise from hours of focused thought.

It occurred to her in an instant, based on months, even years, of background work by her brain's default network. After making countless neural connections, searching for a way to make better sense of René's life, her "little daemons" arrived at Eureka! The P3 wave of thought erupted into her consciousness, and a new idea was born.

Now the Narrator had a new, more empowering storyline for René's life. This enabled her to think differently about herself and the world she inhabited. This new story is truer both to herself and to the actual facts of her life. And it produced a transformation. She began to see herself as a leader, both in her industry and among businesswomen. And that's what she is today.

There are many takeaways from René's inspiring journey, but perhaps the most important is this: You are not stuck with the stories you have about yourself. You can train your Narrator to create a newer, truer storyline for your life.

Creative Writing 101

That's essentially what I (Megan) did when I determined to embrace public speaking as part of my role in our company. I got on board with the idea when I realized that speaking would be an invaluable tool in my leadership role, and that backing away would limit my success. That was a fairly straightforward decision hammered out by my prefrontal cortex and me.

My Narrator, however, was not on board. For years, it had been filling my head with fear about all the terrible things that could happen if I opened my mouth in public. *You'll choke. People will laugh. You'll be embarrassed. You'll flub your words. It'll be a train wreck. Everybody will be watching.* As you can see, the Narrator majors on fear and is very persuasive.

For several weeks, I tried to retrain my Narrator by repeating the affirmations I mentioned earlier. That worked to some degree. My anxiety level was gradually decreasing.

Then, the day before my speech, my Narrator fought back and hit me with an all-out attack, telling the old stories about fear and failure. And it worked. I had a full-on breakdown after

You are not stuck with the stories you have about yourself. You can train your Narrator to create a newer, truer storyline for your life.

my last sound check—a panic attack, ugly crying, planning my escape from the country, the works. I was afraid of disgracing my team, tarnishing the family name, destroying the company, embarrassing myself. It was a complete mess.

Fortunately, my sister Mary was able to talk me off the ledge. Over the next day, she played stand-in for my Narrator, filling my mind with positive stories not based on fear. I regained my composure, got some sleep, and then delivered my speech exactly as I'd envisioned it.

Here's the interesting thing: my Narrator had no answer for that. I'd placed a big fat achievement smack in the middle of its story of fear and failure. And it had no comeback. The old story didn't make sense anymore—I had written a new one.

I've had to speak several times since then. I still get nervous. Sometimes I feel self-conscious about it and my chest flushes scarlet. But mostly I laugh it off and speak anyway. It's easier because my Narrator has different material to work with when it feeds me storylines. Instead of failure and fear, my memory is full of scenes of successful delivery with grateful audiences. And that's the story my Narrator tells me now.

For many of us, the things we want most are on the other side of discomfort. And no one feels that discomfort more acutely than our Narrator. Yet by taking one step at a time, adding new experiences to our library, we give our Narrator better material to work with, and it presents us with better stories.

As E. L. Doctorow said, writing a novel is like "driving a car at night. You never see further than your headlights, but you can make the whole trip that way."[1] Life is like that too. You just tackle one mildly scary step at a time, and you keep repeating until you get there. Each step gives your Narrator one more hopeful line to include in your next story.

Reading Aloud

I (Michael) learned another tactic for retraining my Narrator after being confronted by my executive coach to evaluate how my leadership affects outcomes.

Aside from forcing me to take ownership of the results in my business, that moment opened my eyes to the narratives that had driven my thoughts, emotions, and actions. Without realizing it, I was taking my Narrator's storyline as absolute fact in every area of my life. Because I was completely unaware of these stories, it never occurred to me that I could question them.

When sales were down, I blamed the economy. When I had a health problem, I believed it was normal for someone my age. If I was fatigued, I told myself there was nothing I could do to change my energy level. I believed all these stories as if they were gospel.

After being challenged by my coach, I began to notice these stories in nearly every area of my life. Without realizing it, I'd taken a passive stance toward many of the problems I faced because my Narrator told me, "There's nothing you can do about that."

Now my eyes were open to the role of the Narrator and the stories that drove my decisions. I was able to examine these stories and question them. I began an internal dialogue about where they originated from, whether they were true, and why I believed them. I actually stated them out loud and wrote them down to better understand my own thoughts and feelings. Journaling became an everyday habit for me.

As it turns out, my Narrator was a reliable ally most of the time. But not always. Some of the stories I'd accepted as true simply weren't, or no longer had relevance to my life stage. I began to exercise greater agency over my health, relationships, and business decisions. I was able to edit, rewrite, or simply replace some of the beliefs that had hindered my results.

Today, I am in the best shape of my life. My relationship with my wife is better than it's ever been. And I have achieved more professional satisfaction than I ever dreamed possible. All of that can be traced to the moment when I became aware of the stories I'd tacitly accepted as true.

Reframing Fear

Our potential is bound only by our imagination. When we break free from the stories that limit our potential, we drive progress and achievement. When we interrogate the thoughts our Narrator is feeding us and update them to be more accurate and helpful, we change the course of our lives. Every great innovator has employed some version of this process.

The world is dynamic, not static. We create it fresh each day. Yesterday's magic is tomorrow's meh. What worked then may not work now. That thought can be unsettling, because it runs counter to our natural desire for safety and certainty. We crave stability so that we can know what to expect from day to day, moment to moment. We depend on that sense of certainty for the confidence to take action.

We might think of certainty like having all the LEGO bricks in your world glued in place. Every structure, every relationship, every place would be unmoved and unmovable. That would bring with it some degree of reassurance. Institutions would never falter. Relationships would never devolve. Your world would never fall apart. Neither would it change. In a static world, there would be no new possible combinations, no possibility for improvement, no growth. The same would be true of you.[2]

Uncertainty is intimidating. It breaks up the bricks, destroying or at least calling into question existing structures. We wake each morning knowing that some corner of our world will be different than it was the day before. Unsettling as it may be, uncertainty is not the enemy, for it points not to chaos but to possibility.

IN A WORLD WHERE everything is dynamic, anything is possible. To have the confidence to engage that world and reshape our stories as needed is a far more valuable and reassuring asset than is certainty. Once we accept the inevitability of change, we have no need to remain tied to ineffectual strategies and actions. Instead, we can respond effectively to whatever comes our way. The choice is up to you.

To make that choice will require a change of perspective. We must come to see uncertainty as a lever, not an impediment. Those who can learn to tolerate the temporary discomfort of uncertainty will produce better results in business, in relationships, and in life than will those who insist on applying yesterday's shopworn solutions.

The converse is also true. Those who refuse to engage in the dynamic process of rethinking their approach to life and imagining new solutions will remain stuck. This approach will produce fewer and fewer satisfactory results, greater and greater frustration, and, in the end, the feeling that life has somehow passed them by.

THE CHOICE TO RETHINK our thinking requires us to overcome our fears. This shift in perspective is challenging. It can be terrifying to admit that our stories no longer help us to navigate through life. It's tempting to double down on the stories that have become familiar to us—like René standing at the periphery—even though they no longer describe reality in a meaningful way.

But that's a choice: either we embrace some uncertainty and with it the possibility of change, or we retreat into the worn-out stories that now seem more and more like fiction.

You're not alone in this choice. You are joined by a community of innovative thinkers willing to admit that the answers we need don't yet exist. The best way to proceed is in the company of others who are equally bent on exploring, creating, and becoming.

By choosing to rethink your stories, you are choosing action over passivity. It is always easier to accept the status quo, even when it's not to your liking, because that removes the burden of responsibility. If the world can't be changed, then it's certainly not up to you to change it. When you admit that the way things are is not the way they must be, and that we can change reality by changing the way we think about our problems, the responsibility for change falls—to one degree or another—on us. We must choose to act on the things we care about, to pursue our goals and see them through.

> **By choosing to rethink your stories, you are choosing action over passivity.**

Ultimately, this is a choice to imagine and create a better future for ourselves. That will mean doing the hard work of interrogating our own stories to get a clear, truer picture of the problems at hand. Then we must do the hard, sometimes slow and tedious work of reimagining a new path.

There's Always a Better Story

Hugh Herr, the seventeen-year-old mountain climber and double amputee, had the courage to reimagine his life without legs. You know the result. He was able to reject the story that limited him to sitting at the bottom of the hill. He imagined a new, better set of prosthetic limbs, then created them. He climbed again. That's a great story.

But it was not Herr's final chapter. He went on to study mechanical engineering and biophysics, becoming one of the world's leading developers of bionic prosthetics. He now works at MIT, has developed artificial knees and ankles, and has helped restore mobility to people who never imagined walking, running, or climbing again.

"We've had one fellow lose close to 30 pounds after using the device for a few months because he's walking so much more," says Herr. "Another person doesn't use the handicap placard—so the device has already had deeply profound effects on quality of life."

Even that is not the end of the story. "I predict that as we march into this 21st century, the changes we'll see in prosthetic designs [will be that] the artificial prosthetic will become more intimate with the biological human body," Herr predicts. "The prosthesis will be attached to the body mechanically by a titanium shaft that goes right into the residual bone, wherein you can't take the artificial limb off."

And that's not all. "Another intimate connection will be electrical. The nervous system of the human will be able to communicate directly with the synthetic nervous system of the artificial limb."[3] Who knows what other stories will emerge from Herr's mind?

Or yours.

We offer you this invitation. Accept the challenge of examining your own life. Identify the stories you tell yourself. Interrogate them. Then reimagine them in a way that is truer to your heart and more accurately reflects reality.

Embrace the mindset of possibility. Accept the challenge of uncertainty. Resist the fear that would keep you passive. Commit yourself to a life of transformation and contribution. You will find yourself free to become a different person than you were yesterday, and to achieve things tomorrow that seem impossible today. There is no telling where that story may lead.

OUR THANKS

Writing a book is a case study in what we talked about in chapter 9, using the brains of others. Few of the ideas are original. Most are a synthesis of other concepts. That's particularly true for this book.

Ilene Muething, my (Michael's) executive coach for several years while she was at Gap International, was the first person to help me see the relationship between my thoughts, actions, and outcomes. She insisted that if I want to get different results, I have to think different thoughts. The lesson stuck.

I (Megan) also benefited from coaching with Ilene, along with another coach from Gap, Nancy Sloan. They both have been a huge help to me in understanding how instrumental thinking is to performance.

Likewise, we've both benefited from Brooke Castillo's work, particularly her model for self-coaching, and Leonard Mlodinow's and Mariano Sigman's helpful introductions to brain science. It was seeing the intersection of those two worlds which sparked the idea for this book.

Beyond these, we've learned from so many other writers and thinkers whose names and books are found in the Further Reading suggestions on page 219. As Alan Jacobs—one of those writers—says, "Thinking independently, solitarily, 'for ourselves,' is not an option."[1] We rely on foundations laid, trails blazed, and ideas gathered by others.

And speaking of gathering, Joel Miller, Larry Wilson, and Jessica Rogers brought it all together. I (Michael) have been working with Joel for more than twenty years. We've now collaborated on nine books; I can't imagine a better creative partner. Almost no one is more familiar with our ideas and frameworks than Larry. And Jessica brought her years of editorial expertise to the mix. They did the lion's share of the research and helped synthesize our thinking.

The team at Baker Publishing Group is the dream team as far as publishing goes. Our thanks to Dwight Baker, Brian Vos, and Mark Rice for believing in us. You guys are a joy to work with— same with Barb Barnes and Natalie Nyquist. Also, thanks to Bryan Norman, our literary agent at Alive Communications, for challenging our thinking and championing our cause.

I (Michael) would be remiss if I didn't acknowledge Gail, my wife of more than four decades. She has had a huge impact on my thinking. She is always the first person I share my ideas with. Though she is always quick to encourage me, she is also the one who advocates for greater simplicity and more clarity.

I (Megan) want to call out Joel here as well. Not only is he pretty handy with a book project, he also helps me keep my Narrator in check. He's the best life partner I could imagine.

Finally, we want to thank the entire Full Focus team. Leaving out those already mentioned above, at this writing our team includes DeAnne Anderson, Courtney Baker, Mike "Verbs"

Boyer, Susan Caldwell, Ora Corr, Aleshia Curry, Trey Duna-vant, Andrew Fockel, Natalie Fockel, Antonette Gardner, Dustin Guyton, John Harrison, Brent High, Adam Hill, Marissa Hyatt, Jim Kelly, Hannah Leigh, Elizabeth Lynch, Annie Mayberry, LeeAnn Moody, Renee Murphy, Laura Nelson, Erin Perry, Johnny Poole, Katherine Rowley, Brian Shun, Brian Stachurski, Emi Tanke, Hannah Williamson, and Dave Yankowiak.

They free us up to focus on what we do best. We've never worked with a better team of people.

FURTHER READING

Anyone interested in going deeper with this subject can find plenty of direction in the endnotes, but we'd like to pull out the resources that were most useful to us and include some additional reading that helped us formulate our own thinking. We'll divide these according to the major divisions of the book.

———

Gottschall, Jonathan. *The Storytelling Animal: How Stories Make Us Human*. Boston: Mariner Books, 2012.

Storr, Will. *The Science of Storytelling: Why Stories Make Us Human and How to Tell Them Better*. New York: Abrams Press, 2020.

Identify

Barrett, Lisa Feldman. *How Emotions Are Made: The Secret Life of the Brain*. New York: Mariner Books, 2018.

———. *7½ Lessons about the Brain*. New York: Houghton Mifflin Harcourt, 2020.

Buzsáki, György. *The Brain from Inside Out*. New York: Oxford University Press, 2019.

Dehaene, Stanislas. *Consciousness and the Brain: Deciphering How the Brain Codes Our Thoughts*. New York: Penguin Books, 2014.

———. *How We Learn: Why Brains Learn Better Than Any Machine . . . for Now*. New York: Viking, 2020.

Fleming, Stephen M. *Know Thyself: The Science of Self-Awareness*. New York: Basic Books, 2021.

Frith, Chris. *Making Up the Mind: How Our Brain Creates Our Mental World*. Oxford: Blackwell Publishing, 2007.

Gazzaniga, Michael S. *Human: The Science behind What Makes Your Brain Unique*. New York: Ecco, 2008.

———. *Tales from Both Sides of the Brain: A Life in Neuroscience*. New York: Ecco, 2015.

Goldstein, E. Bruce. *The Mind: Consciousness, Prediction, and the Brain*. Cambridge: MIT Press, 2020.

Lotto, Beau. *Deviate: The Science of Seeing Differently*. New York: Hachette Books, 2017.

Mlodinow, Leonard. *Elastic: Unlocking Your Brain's Ability to Embrace Change*. New York: Vintage Books, 2019.

———. *Subliminal: How Your Unconscious Mind Rules Your Behavior*. New York: Vintage Books, 2013.

Pearl, Judea, and Dana MacKenzie. *The Book of Why: The New Science of Cause and Effect*. New York: Basic Books, 2018.

Ratey, John J. *A User's Guide to the Brain: Perception, Attention, and the Four Theaters of the Brain*. New York: Vintage Books, 2001.

Sigman, Mariano. *The Secret Life of the Mind*. New York: Little, Brown, and Company, 2017.

Tversky, Barbara. *Mind in Motion: How Action Shapes Thought*. New York: Basic Books, 2019.

Interrogate

Bargh, John. *Before You Know It: The Unconscious Reasons We Do What We Do*. New York: Atria Paperback, 2017.

Blastland, Michael. *The Hidden Half: How the World Conceals Its Secrets*. London: Atlantic Books, 2019.

Jacobs, Alan. *How to Think: A Survival Guide for a World at Odds*. New York: Currency, 2017.

Kahneman, Daniel. *Thinking, Fast and Slow*. New York: Farrar, Straus & Giroux, 2011.

Kastor, Deena, and Michelle Hamilton. *Let Your Mind Run: A Memoir of Thinking My Way to Victory*. New York: Three Rivers Press, 2019.

Lakhoff, George, and Mark Johnson. *Metaphors We Live By*. Chicago: University of Chicago Press, 1980.

Macdonald, Hector. *Truth: How the Many Sides to Every Story Shape Our Reality*. New York: Little, Brown Spark, 2018.

Robson, David. *The Intelligence Trap: Why Smart People Make Dumb Mistakes*. New York: Norton, 2019.

Schulz, Kathryn. *Being Wrong: Adventures on the Margin of Error*. New York: Ecco, 2011.

Sibony, Olivier. *You're About to Make a Terrible Mistake: How Biases Distort Decision-Making—and What You Can Do to Fight Them*. Translated by Kate Deimling. New York: Little, Brown Spark, 2020.

Watts, Duncan J. *Everything Is Obvious: Once You Know the Answer*. New York: Crown Business, 2011.

Imagine

Boaler, Jo. *Limitless Mind: Learn, Lead, and Live without Barriers*. San Francisco: HarperOne, 2019.

Bouquet, Cyril, Jean-Louis Barsou, and Michael Wade. *A.L.I.E.N. Thinking: The Unconventional Path to Breakthrough Ideas*. New York: Public Affairs, 2021.

Eagleman, David, and Anthony Brandt. *The Runaway Species: How Human Creativity Remakes the World*. New York: Catapult, 2017.

Goldberg, Elkhonon. *Creativity: The Human Brain in the Age of Innovation*. New York: Oxford University Press, 2018.

Grant, Adam. *Think Again: The Power of Knowing What You Don't Know*. New York: Viking, 2021.

Heffernan, Margaret. *Uncharted: How to Navigate the Future*. New York: Avid Reader Press, 2020.

Johnson, Steven. *Where Good Ideas Come From: The Natural History of Innovation*. New York: Riverhead Books, 2010.

Kaufman, Scott Barry, and Carolyn Gregoire. *Wired to Create: Unraveling the Mysteries of the Creative Mind*. New York: TarcherPerigee, 2015.

Klein, Gary. *Seeing What Others Don't: The Remarkable Ways We Gain Insights*. New York: Public Affairs, 2013.

Luca, Michael, and Max H. Bazerman. *The Power of Experiments: Decision Making in a Data-Driven World*. Cambridge, Mass.: MIT Press, 2020.

Martin, Roger. *The Opposable Mind: How Successful Leaders Win through Integrative Thinking*. Boston: Harvard Business Review Press, 2007.

Paul, Anna Murphy. *The Extended Mind: The Power of Thinking Outside the Brain*. Boston: Houghton Mifflin Harcourt, 2021.

Postrel, Virginia. *The Future and Its Enemies: The Growing Conflict over Creativity, Enterprise, and Progress*. New York: Touchstone, 1999.

Ratey, John J., with Eric Hagerman. *Spark: The Revolutionary New Science of Exercise and the Brain*. New York: Little, Brown Spark, 2008.

Riel, Jennifer, and Roger Martin. *Creating Great Choices: A Leader's Guide to Integrative Thinking*. Boston: Harvard Business Review Press, 2017.

Sloman, Steven, and Philip Fernbach. *The Illusion of Knowledge: Why We Never Think Alone*. New York: Riverhead Books, 2017.

Thomke, Stefan H. *Experimentation Works: The Surprising Power of Business Experiments*. Boston: Harvard Business Review Press, 2020.

NOTES

Chapter 1 The Brain That Tells Itself Stories

1. See Bessel A. van der Kolk, *The Body Keeps the Score* (New York: Penguin, 2014).

2. See, for example, the recommendations in Karyn B. Purvis et al., *The Connected Child* (New York: McGraw Hill, 2007), 197–211.

3. Sebern Fisher, *Neurofeedback and the Treatment of Developmental Trauma* (New York: Norton, 2014).

4. Daniel J. Siegel is an important thinker and practitioner regarding the intersection of mind and narrative. See, for instance, chap. 31 ("Narrative") in his book *The Pocket Guide to Interpersonal Neurobiology* (New York: Norton, 2012).

5. Neuron counts range from 86 billion to 128 billion. Why the discrepancy? It all comes down to how scientists do the counting. We'll be rounding our number to 100 billion. For more on this, see Lisa Feldman Barrett, *7½ Lessons about the Brain* (New York: Houghton Mifflin Harcourt, 2020), 147; and Carl Zimmer, "100 Trillion Connections: New Efforts Probe and Map the Brain's Detailed Architecture," *Scientific American*, January 2011, https://www.scientificamerican.com/article/100-trillion-connections/.

6. Beau Lotto, *Deviate: The Science of Seeing Differently* (New York: Hachette, 2017), 159.

7. Steven Johnson, *Where Good Ideas Come From: The Natural History of Innovation* (New York: Riverhead Books, 2010), 46.

8. Timothy D. Wilson, *Redirect: Changing the Stories We Live By* (New York: Back Bay Books, 2015), 71.

9. We should add that this is not in lieu of professional help. But if you have smaller-scale issues you can address on your own, this is an excellent way to do it that works in conjunction with professional help.

Chapter 2 Introducing the Narrator

1. Judea Pearl and Dana Mackenzie, *The Book of Why: The New Science of Cause and Effect* (New York: Basic Books, 2018), 24.

2. Quotations from Genesis 3:9–13.

3. Pearl and Mackenzie, *Book of Why*, 24.

4. Angus Fletcher, "Why Computers Will Never Read (or Write) Literature," *Narrative* 29, no. 1 (January 2021): 1–28. See also Angus Fletcher, "Why Computers Will Never Write Good Novels," *Nautilus*, February 10, 2021, https://nautil.us/issue/95/escape/why-computers-will-never-write -good-novels.

5. Leonard Mlodinow, *Elastic: Unlocking Your Brain's Ability to Embrace Change* (New York: Pantheon, 2018), 78.

6. Mlodinow, *Elastic*, 78. See also Rodrigo Quian Quiroga, "Concept Cells: The Building Blocks of Declarative Memory Functions," *Nature Reviews Neuroscience* 13 (2012): 587–97, https://doi.org/10.1038 /nrn3251.

7. György Buzsáki, *The Brain from Inside Out* (New York: Oxford University Press, 2019), 104, 189, 347.

8. Mlodinow, *Elastic*, 78.

9. Paul Harris, as cited in Ian Leslie, *Curious: The Desire to Know and Why Your Future Depends on It* (New York: Basic Books, 2015), 28.

10. Elkhonon Goldberg, *Creativity: The Human Brain in the Age of Innovation* (New York: Oxford University Press, 2018), 36.

11. Matthew Cobb, *The Idea of the Brain: The Past and Future of Neuroscience* (New York: Basic Books, 2020), 344–47. See also Jonathan Gotschall, *Storytelling Animal: How Stories Make Us Human* (Boston: Mariner Books, 2012), 97.

12. Michael S. Gazzaniga, *Tales from Both Sides of the Brain: A Life in Neuroscience* (New York: Ecco, 2015), 150.

13. Gazzaniga, *Tales from Both Sides of the Brain*, 151.

14. Gazzaniga, *Tales from Both Sides of the Brain*, 153. See also Michael S. Gazzaniga, *Human: The Science behind What Makes Your Brain Unique* (New York: Harper Perennial, 2008), 294–300.

15. Gazzaniga named this function of the brain the Interpreter. To underscore the connection to what we're calling the Narrator, remember what

historian Albert Raboteau says: "Narration is . . . an act of interpretation." The Narrator/Interpreter is the sense-making function of the brain.

16. Mark Michaud, "Study Reveals Brain's Finely Tuned System of Energy Supply," University of Rochester Medical Center, August 7, 2016, https://www.urmc.rochester.edu/news/story/study-reveals-brains-finely -tuned-system-of-energy-supply.

17. Jon Hamilton, "Think You're Multitasking? Think Again," October 2, 2008, in *Morning Edition*, NPR, MP3 audio, 21:07, https://www.npr .org/templates/story/story.php?storyId=95256794.

18. Stanislas Dehaene, *Consciousness and the Brain: Deciphering How the Brain Codes Our Thoughts* (New York: Penguin Books, 2014), 176.

19. Dehaene, *Consciousness and the Brain*, chap. 4 ("The Signatures of a Conscious Thought").

20. Dehaene, *Consciousness and the Brain*, 125.

21. Lisa Feldman Barrett, *How Emotions Are Made: The Secret Life of the Brain* (New York: Mariner Books, 2018), 28; Goldberg, *Creativity*, 84.

22. See Chris Frith, *Making Up the Mind: How the Brain Creates Our Mental World* (Malden, MA: Blackwell, 2007); and Andy Clark, *Surfing Uncertainty: Prediction, Action, and the Embodied Mind* (Oxford: Oxford University Press, 2016).

Chapter 3 How Your Brain Shapes Stories

1. Buzsáki, *The Brain from Inside Out*, 127–28.

2. Bret Stetka, "Our Brain Uses a Not-So-Instant Replay to Make Decisions," *Scientific American*, June 27, 2019, https://www.scientificamerican .com/article/our-brain-uses-a-not-so-instant-replay-to-make-decisions.

3. Buzsáki, *Brain*, 122, 124.

4. Buzsáki, *Brain*, 124.

5. Buzsáki, *Brain*, 126.

6. Frank Schaeffer, *Crazy for God* (New York: Da Capo, 2008), 6.

7. Philip Roth, *The Facts: A Novelist's Autobiography* (New York: Vintage International, 1997), 8.

8. S. I. Hayakawa and Alan Hayakawa, *Language in Thought and Action* (New York: Harcourt, 1990), 19.

9. Alan Jacobs, *How to Think: A Survival Guide for a World at Odds* (New York: Currency, 2018), 39.

10. Nicholas A. Christakis and James H. Fowler, "The Spread of Obesity in a Large Social Network over 32 Years," *The New England Journal of Medicine* 357, no. 4 (2007): 370–79, https://www.nejm.org/doi/full/10

.1056/NEJMsa066082; and Nicholas A. Christakis and James H. Fowler, "The Collective Dynamics of Smoking in a Large Social Network," *The New England Journal of Medicine* 358, no. 21 (2008): 2249–58, nejm.org/doi /full/10.1056/NEJMsa0706154.

11. James H. Fowler and Nicholas A. Christakis, "Dynamic Spread of Happiness in a Large Social Network: Longitudinal Analysis over 20 Years in the Framingham Heart Study," *BMJ* 337 (2008): a2338, https://www .bmj.com/content/337/bmj.a2338.

12. Jacobs, *How to Think*, 87.

13. Steven Sloman and Philip Fernbach, *The Knowledge Illusion: Why We Never Think Alone* (New York: Riverhead, 2017), 13.

14. Robert A. Burton, "Our Brains Tell Stories So We Can Live," *Nautilus*, August 8, 2019, https://nautil.us/issue/75/story/our-brains-tell-stories -so-we-can-live.

15. Lotto, *Deviate*, 159–60.

16. Lotto, *Deviate*, 38–40.

Chapter 4 Your Brain's Big Project

1. Jennifer Griffin Graham (@jgriffingraham), "My kid discovered you can photocopy anything and now he's trying to prank me," Twitter, July 17, 2021, 4:03 p.m., https://twitter.com/jgriffingraham/status /1416488778122866690; "5-Year-Old Kid Pranks Mother with 'Photocopy' of Socks, Twitter Left in Splits," News18, July 20, 2021, https://www .news18.com/news/buzz/5-year-old-kid-pranks-mother-with-photocopy -of-socks-twitter-left-in-splits-3983990.html.

2. "The Treachery of Images, 1929 by Rene Magritte," Rene Magritte: Biography, Painting, and Quotes (website), https://www.renemagritte.org /the-treachery-of-images.jsp.

3. Lotto, *Deviate*, 61.

4. David Deutsch, *Fabric of Reality: The Science of Parallel Universes—and Its Implications* (New York: Penguin Books, 1997), 121.

5. Buzsáki, *Brain*, 104. See also, as mentioned above, Frith, *Making Up the Mind*, and Clark, *Surfing Uncertainty*.

6. Deutsch, *Fabric of Reality*, 121.

7. Frith, *Making Up the Mind*, 132–35.

8. Kenneth Craik, *The Nature of Explanation* (Cambridge, UK: Cambridge University Press, 1943), 56. See also Cobb, *Idea of the Brain*, 185.

9. Cobb, *Idea of the Brain*, 185; and Buzsáki, *Brain*, 102.

10. Running alternate stories in our minds allows us to test a hundred different strategies without significant consequences, whereas any one of

them in actuality might be dangerous or destructive. "Let our conjectures . . . die in our stead," said philosopher of science Karl Popper, who is famous for another quip: "Good tests kill flawed theories; we remain alive to guess again."

11. Buzsáki, *Brain*, 347.

12. Buzsáki, *Brain*, 347.

13. Pearl and Mackenzie, *Book of Why*, 22–27.

14. Barbara Tversky, *Mind in Motion: How Action Shapes Thought* (New York: Basic Books, 2019), 78, 244.

15. Mariano Sigman, *The Secret Life of the Mind* (New York: Little, Brown, and Company, 2017), 76; Leonard Mlodinow, *Subliminal: How Your Unconscious Mind Rules Your Behavior* (New York: Pantheon, 2012), 89.

16. Goldberg, *Creativity*, 161.

17. For more on this, see Stephen M. Fleming, "A Theory of My Own Mind," *Aeon*, September 23, 2021, https://aeon.co/essays/is-there-a-symmetry-between-metacognition-and-mindreading. See also Stephen M. Fleming, *Know Thyself: The Science of Self-Awareness* (New York: Basic Books, 2021), 55–74.

18. Barrett, *How Emotions Are Made*, 28.

19. Alison Osius, *Second Ascent: The Story of Hugh Herr* (New York: Laurel, 1993), 129.

20. "The Double Amputee Who Designs Better Limbs," interview with Hugh Herr, *Fresh Air*, NPR, August 10, 2011, https://www.npr.org/transcripts/137552538.

21. Osius, *Second Ascent*, 146.

22. Osius, *Second Ascent*, 149; "Double Amputee," *Fresh Air*; Eric Adelson, "Best Foot Forward," *Boston*, February 18, 2009, https://www.boston magazine.com/2009/02/18/best-foot-forward-february/.

Chapter 5 Separating Fact from Fiction

1. Krista Tippett, "Mary Karr: Astonished by the Comedy," *On Being with Krista Tippett*, October 13, 2016, produced by Chris Heagle and Zack Rose, podcast, 52:09, https://onbeing.org/programs/mary-karr-astonished-by-the-human-comedy-jan2018.

2. Barrett, *How Emotions Are Made*. See especially chaps. 2 ("Emotions Are Constructed"), 4 ("The Origin of Feeling"), and 6 ("How the Brain Makes Emotion").

3. Carl R. Rogers, *On Becoming a Person* ([1961] New York: Houghton Mifflin, 1995), 25.

4. Joanna Blythman, "Can Vegans Stomach the Unpalatable Truth about Quinoa?" *Guardian*, Jan. 16, 2013, https://www.theguardian.com/commentisfree/2013/jan/16/vegans-stomach-unpalatable-truth-quinoa.

5. Hector MacDonald, *Truth: How the Many Sides to Every Story Shape Our Reality* (New York: Little, Brown Spark, 2018), 2.

6. Buzsáki, *Brain*, 44.

7. Michael Blastland, *The Hidden Half: How the World Conceals Its Secrets* (London: Atlantic Books, 2019).

8. James Geary, *I Is an Other: The Secret Life of Metaphor and How It Shapes the Way We See the World* (New York: Harper Perennial, 2011), 5.

9. George Lakoff and Mark Johnson, *Metaphors We Live By* (Chicago: University of Chicago Press, 2003), 156.

10. David Robertson with Bill Breen, *Brick by Brick: How LEGO Rewrote the Rules of Innovation and Conquered the Global Toy Industry* (New York: Crown Business, 2013), 44ff.

11. Blastland, *The Hidden Half*. See especially chap. 3 ("Here Is Not There, Then Is Not Now") and 5 ("The Principle Isn't Practical").

12. Blastland, *Hidden Half*, 81.

13. For more on this distinction, see Michael Strevens, *The Knowledge Machine* (New York: Liveright, 2020).

Chapter 6 The Ups and Downs of Intuition

1. University of Leeds, "Go with Your Gut—Intuition Is More Than Just a Hunch, Says New Research," ScienceDaily, March 6, 2008, http://www.sciencedaily.com/releases/2008/03/080305144210.htm.

2. Buzsáki, *Brain*, 91.

3. University of Leeds, "Go with Your Gut."

4. René Descartes, *Key Philosophical Writings* (Ware, UK: Wordsworth Editions, 1997), 31.

5. Wayne P. Pomerleau, *Twelve Great Philosophers: A Historical Introduction to Human Nature* (New York: Ardsley House, 1997), 243.

6. Martin Robson and Peter Miller, "Australian Elite Leaders and Intuition," *Australasian Journal of Business and Social Inquiry* 4, no. 3 (2006): 43–61, https://researchportal.scu.edu.au/discovery/fulldisplay/alma991012820835502368/61SCU_INST:ResearchRepository.

7. Annie Murphy Paul, *The Extended Mind: The Power of Thinking Outside the Brain* (Boston: Houghton Mifflin Harcourt, 2021), 21.

8. John Bargh, *Before You Know It: The Unconscious Reasons We Do What We Do* (New York: Atria Paperback, 2017), 165.

9. University of Leeds, "Go with Your Gut."

10. Elena Lytkina Botelho et al., "What Sets Successful CEOs Apart," *Harvard Business Review*, May–June 2017, https://hbr.org/2017/05/what -sets-successful-ceos-apart.

11. Bargh, *Before You Know It*, 157, 173.

Chapter 7 Trading Certainty for Results

1. Chris Mellor, "Three Years In: Can Kurian Heal Sickly NetApp's Woes?," *The Register*, July 7, 2016, https://www.theregister.com/2016/07 /07/george_kurian_reviving_netapps_zing/.

2. Martin J. Smith, "The Importance of Embracing Uncertainty," *Insights*, November 6, 2017, https://www.gsb.stanford.edu/insights/importance -embracing-uncertainty.

3. Amy Reichelt, "Your Brain on Sugar: What the Science Actually Says," The Conversation, November 14, 2019, https://theconversation.com/your -brain-on-sugar-what-the-science-actually-says-126581.

4. Søren Kierkegaard, *The Sickness Unto Death: A Christian Psychological Exposition for Upbuilding and Awakening*, trans. Howard V. Hong and Edna H. Hong (Princeton: Princeton University Press, 1980), 41.

5. Barna, "Americans Feel Good," Barna.com, February 27, 2018, https:// www.barna.com/research/americans-feel-good-counseling/.

6. Karl Hille, "Hubble Reveals Observable Universe Contains 10 Times More Galaxies Than Previously Thought," NASA, October 13, 2016, https:// www.nasa.gov/feature/goddard/2016/hubble-reveals-observable-universe -contains-10-times-more-galaxies-than-previously-thought.

7. See, for instance, C. S. Lewis's "Illustrations of the Tao" in *The Abolition of Man* (New York: HarperOne), 83–101.

8. G. K. Chesterton, *Orthodoxy* (Mineola, NY: Dover Publications, 2020), 25.

9. Al Pittampalli, *Persuadable: How Great Leaders Change Their Minds to Change the World* (New York: HarperCollins, 2016), 6.

Chapter 8 Different Neurons Tell Different Stories

1. Buzsáki, *Brain*, 337–38.

2. Buzsáki, *Brain*, 338.

3. Mlodinow, *Elastic*, 95. Jacobs also discusses this relational aspect of thinking in *How to Think*.

4. Jo Boaler, *Limitless Mind: Learn, Lead, and Live without Barriers* (San Francisco: HarperOne, 2019), 3.

5. See Christopher Hitchens's comments about living "as if" in *Letters to a Young Contrarian* (New York: Basic Books, 2001), 35–39.

6. Martin E. P. Seligman, *Learned Optimism: How to Change Your Mind and Your Life* (New York: Vintage Books, 2006).

7. Goldberg, *Creativity*, 158.

8. Gary Klein, *Seeing What Others Don't: The Remarkable Ways We Gain Insights* (New York: Public Affairs, 2013), 61–77.

9. Loizos Heracleous and David Robson, "Why the 'Paradox Mindset' Is the Key to Success," *Worklife*, BBC, November 11, 2020, https://www.bbc.com/worklife/article/20201109-why-the-paradox-mindset-is-the-key-to-success.

10. For more on this, see Margaret Cuonzo, *Paradox* (Cambridge, MA: MIT Press, 2014).

11. For more on this, see Jennifer Riel and Roger Martin, *Creating Great Choices: A Leader's Guide to Integrative Thinking* (Boston: Harvard Business Review Press, 2017).

12. Goldberg, *Creativity*, 164.

13. Heracleous and Robson, "'Paradox Mindset.'"

14. Dan Kois, "Good News: Our Children Have Some Terrific Ideas for How to Get the Big Ol' Boat Unstuck from the Suez Canal," *Slate*, March 25, 2021, https://slate.com/news-and-politics/2021/03/cargo-ship-stuck-in-the-suez-canal-children-have-ideas-for-how-to-move-it.html.

15. Stefan Mumaw, "The Shape of Ideation," TEDx Talks, June 5, 2015, https://www.youtube.com/watch?v=BErt2qRmoFQ.

16. Mumaw, "Shape of Ideation."

17. See, e.g., Klein, *Seeing What Others Don't*; David Eagleman and Anthony Brandt, *The Runaway Species: How Human Creativity Remakes the World* (New York: Catapult, 2017); and Armand D'Angour, "Introduction," in Aristotle, *How to Innovate* (Princeton: Princeton University Press, 2021), esp. p. xvi.

18. Nitin Nohria and Michael Beer, "Cracking the Code of Change," *Harvard Business Review*, May–June 2000, https://hbr.org/2000/05/cracking-the-code-of-change.

19. Margaret Heffernan, *Uncharted: How to Navigate the Future* (New York: Avid Reader Press, 2020), chap. 4 ("No Available Datasets").

20. Michael Luca and Max H. Bazerman, *The Power of Experiments: Decision Making in a Data-Driven World* (Cambridge, MA: MIT Press, 2020), 114–20.

21. Stanislas Dehaene, *How We Learn: Why Brains Learn Better Than Any Machine . . . for Now* (New York: Viking, 2020), 205.

22. Dehaene, *How We Learn*, 205.

23. The source of this quip is likely Nobel-winning economist Ronald Coase, famous for his Coase Theorem. See the comparable line in R. H. Coase, *Essays on Economics and Economists* (Chicago: University of Chicago Press, 1995), 27.

24. Ivar Giaever, "Electron Tunneling and Superconductivity," Nobel Lecture, December 12, 1973, https://www.nobelprize.org/uploads/2018/06/giaever-lecture.pdf.

25. René Redzepi, *A Work in Progress: A Journal* (New York: Phaidon, 2018), 92.

26. Redzepi, *Work in Progress*, 171.

27. Redzepi, *Work in Progress*, 102. See also Jeff Gordinier, *Hungry: Eating, Road-Tripping, and Risking It All with the Greatest Chef in the World* (New York: Tim Duggan, 2019).

Chapter 9 More Brains Are Better Than One

1. Michael Pollak, "Einstein Groupies," *New York Times*, August 10, 2012, https://www.nytimes.com/2012/08/12/nyregion/dissecting-the-einstein-riot-of-1930.html.

2. Frederic Golden, "Albert Einstein," *TIME*, December 31, 1999, http://content.time.com/time/magazine/article/0,9171,993017,00.html.

3. Walter Isaacson, *Einstein: His Life and Universe* (New York: Simon & Schuster, 2008), 509.

4. Isaacson, *Einstein*, 519.

5. Michio Kaku, *Einstein's Cosmos: How Albert Einstein's Vision Transformed Our Understanding of Space* (New York: Norton, 2005), 46.

6. David Bodanis, *Einstein's Greatest Mistake: A Biography* (New York: Houghton Mifflin Harcourt, 2016).

7. Kenneth Mikkelsen and Harold Jarche, "The Best Leaders Are Constant Learners," *Harvard Business Review*, October 16, 2015, https://hbr.org/2015/10/the-best-leaders-are-constant-learners.

8. Anders Ericsson and Robert Pool, *Peak: Secrets from the New Science of Expertise* (New York: Houghton Mifflin Harcourt, 2016).

9. See Eli Pariser, *The Filter Bubble: How the New Personalized Web Is Changing How We Think* (New York: Penguin, 2011), chap. 4 ("The You Loop").

10. Jon Gertner, *The Idea Factory: Bell Labs and the Great Age of American Innovation* (New York: Penguin, 2012).

11. Jan Smedslund, "The Invisible Obvious: Culture in Psychology," ed. by Kirsti M. J. Lagerspetz and Pekka Niemi, *Advances in Psychology* 18 (1984): 443–52.

12. Duncan J. Watts, *Everything Is Obvious: Once You Know the Answer* (New York: Crown Business, 2011), chap. 1 ("The Myth of Common Sense").

13. Jean-Louis Barsoux, Cyril Bouquet, and Michael Wade, "Why Outsider Perspectives Are Critical for Innovative Breakthroughs," *MIT Sloan Management Review*, February 8, 2022, https://sloanreview.mit.edu/article/why-outside-perspectives-are-critical-for-innovation-breakthroughs/.

14. Barsoux et al. "Why Outsider Perspectives Are Critical."

15. Barsoux et al. "Why Outsider Perspectives Are Critical."

16. Scott E. Page, *The Diversity Bonus: How Great Teams Pay Off in the Knowledge Economy* (Princeton: Princeton University Press, 2017).

Chapter 10 Let Your Mind Run

1. Thomas S. Kuhn, *The Road Since Structure: Philosophical Essays, 1970–1993 with an Autobiographical Interview* (Chicago: University of Chicago Press, 2000), 16.

2. Buzsáki, *Brain*, 210.

3. Goldberg, *Creativity*, 128.

4. Goldberg, *Creativity*, 128.

5. Mlodinow, *Elastic*, 119.

6. Mlodinow, *Elastic*, 144.

7. Goldberg, *Creativity*, 51, 132.

8. Goldberg, *Creativity*, 95.

9. Buzsáki, *Brain*, 338.

10. Giorgio Vasari, *The Lives of the Artists*, trans. Julia Conaway Bondanella and Peter Bondanella (Oxford: Oxford University Press, 2008), 290. See also Mlodinow, *Elastic*, 126–27.

11. Nancy Coover Andreasen, quoted in Mlodinow, *Elastic*, 121.

12. Goldberg, *Creativity*, 131–32, 138.

13. Goldberg, *Creativity*, 135.

14. Goldberg, *Creativity*, 131–32.

15. Brian McCullough, *How the Internet Happened* (New York: Liveright, 2018), 184–87.

16. Raquel Burrows et al., "Scheduled Physical Activity Is Associated with Better Academic Performance in Chilean School-Age Children," *Journal of Physical Activity and Health* 11 no. 8 (2014): 1600–1606, https://doi.org/10.1123/jpah.2013-0125.

17. John J. Ratey, with Eric Hagerman, *Spark: The Revolutionary New Science of Exercise and the Brain* (New York: Little, Brown Spark, 2008), 5.

18. Ratey, *Spark*, 5.

19. Ratey, *Spark*, 51.

20. Mlodinow, *Elastic*, 146.

21. Matthew Walker, *Why We Sleep: Unlocking the Power of Sleep and Dreams* (New York: Scribner, 2017).

22. Johnson, *Good Ideas*, 31.

Chapter 11 Making the Narrator Your Ally

1. George Plimpton, "E. L. Doctorow, The Art of Fiction No. 94," *Paris Review* 101, Winter 1986, https://www.theparisreview.org/interviews /2718/the-art-of-fiction-no-94-e-l-doctorow.

2. Eagleman and Brandt, *Runaway Species*, chap. 7 ("Don't Glue the Pieces Down").

3. "The Double Amputee Who Designs Better Limbs," *Fresh Air*. For more on Herr and his accomplishments, see also Frank Moss, *The Sorcerers and Their Apprentices* (New York: Crown Business, 2011).

Our Thanks

1. Jacobs, *How to Think*, 39.

INDEX

ABOUT *the* AUTHORS

Michael Hyatt is the founder and chairman of Full Focus, previously Michael Hyatt & Company. Under his leadership, Michael Hyatt & Company has been featured in the Inc. 5000 list of the fastest-growing companies in America for three years in a row. He is also the author of several *New York Times*, *Wall Street Journal*, and *USA Today* bestselling books, including *Platform*, *Living Forward*, *Your Best Year Ever*, *Free to Focus*, and *The Vision Driven Leader*. With his daughter Megan, he is coauthor of *Win at Work and Succeed at Life*. He's living the Double Win with his wife of forty-plus years, five daughters, and nine grandchildren.

Megan Hyatt Miller is the president and chief executive officer of Full Focus. Cohost of the popular business podcast *Lead to Win*, she is also Michael's oldest daughter and coauthor with him of *Win at Work and Succeed at Life*. As the architect of Full Focus's standout culture, she is committed to helping her team win at work and succeed at life, while also delivering phenomenal results to their customers. When she's not taking the company to new heights, she's fully present at home with her husband and five kids in Franklin, Tennessee.

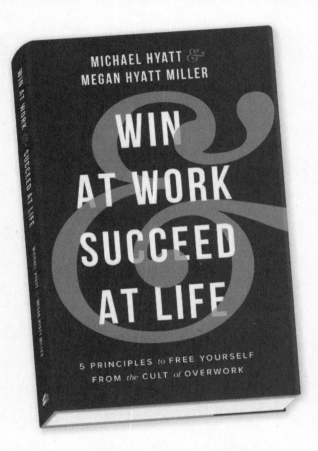

LEADING WITH VISION
CHANGES EVERYTHING

How do you craft a vision? How do you get others on board? And how do you put that vision into practice at every level of your organization? Michael Hyatt asks ten simple questions to help you

- craft an irresistible vision for your business
- ensure it's clear, inspiring, and practical
- rally your team around the vision
- distill it into actionable plans that drive results
- overcome obstacles and pivot as needed

CLOSE THE GAP BETWEEN REALITY
AND YOUR DREAMS

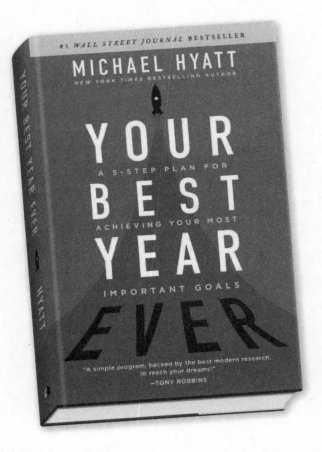

Discover a powerful, proven, research-backed process for setting and achieving life-changing goals.

Focus on What *Matters Most*

Say goodbye to the never-ending to-do list that leads nowhere. The Full Focus Planner is Full Focus's bestselling physical planner to help you set goals and focus on the work that matters.

Plan your
annual goals.

Break them up into
weekly objectives.

Set daily targets
to stay productive
and focused.

GO TO **FULLFOCUSPLANNER.COM** TO CHOOSE
THE PLANNER THAT FITS YOUR LIFESTYLE.